"The Roadmap to a Life Well-Lived"

A NOVEL

DR. VIJENDER CHANDEL

BLUEROSE PUBLISHERS
India | U.K.

Copyright © Dr Vijender Chandel 2023

All rights reserved by author. No part of this publication may be reproduced, stored in a retrieval system or transmitted in any form or by any means, electronic, mechanical, photocopying, recording or otherwise, without the prior permission of the author. Although every precaution has been taken to verify the accuracy of the information contained herein, the publisher assumes no responsibility for any errors or omissions. No liability is assumed for damages that may result from the use of information contained within.

BlueRose Publishers takes no responsibility for any damages, losses, or liabilities that may arise from the use or misuse of the information, products, or services provided in this publication.

For permissions requests or inquiries regarding this publication, please contact:

BLUEROSE PUBLISHERS
www.BlueRoseONE.com
info@bluerosepublishers.com
+91 8882 898 898
+4407342408967

ISBN: 978-93-5989-241-2

Cover design: Muskan Sachdeva
Typesetting: Rohit

First Edition: December 2023

Acknowledgements

First of all, I express my sincere gratitude to Almighty God by whose graces have been able to complete the present task.

There are number of individuals who I would like to acknowledge for their contributions throughout my work, and ultimately to complete this. First, I wish to thank His Excellency Dalai lama and guide, for sharing the knowledge and experience with me, and in so doing, helping me to become a stronger writer, researcher, and individual. It is great pleasure to acknowledge my indebtedness and heartfelt thanks to him. It has, indeed been a very pleasant and rewarding experience to work under his valuable advices.

I am also thankful to all teachers and Principals who gave me full co-operation while I was completing this work.

This work would not be complete without thanking my Himachal Pradesh Government that provided me the opportunity to serve me as Liaison Officer.

I have also searched some ideas from Google, I have also mentioned the things of many people, I am grateful to them too. But I have not mentioned their names.

I express my appreciation to all the knowledgeable persons and personalities, authors and authorities whose ideas, actual quotations have been quoted in the present work.

Dr. Vijender Chandel

Preface

I am grateful to the God who gave me an opportunity to meet with His Excellency the Dalai Lama, not once but eight times. Many topics were discussed His Excellency Dalai lama during the meetings with him.

I've written this book, because lots of people are facing problems. Everyone seems to be upset.

Stress, Depression, Anxiety….all seems to be one of the biggest challenges facing the Youth today, why is it so? People everywhere in the whole world are being asked these questions and trying to find out the solution.

This book is mainly centered on these questions. In fact, Anxiety and depression; serious mental stress is a fact of life for many people in the present age. When we choose happiness in the wrong place that becomes the cause of our suffering and our miseries. Hence, by using our intellect, we can analyze the real position and understand where the real happiness lies that will satisfy us.

How to control our emotions, how to apply the theory of Let-Go, the present Education system has given more stress on material values and has ignored value based education and moral values.

I tried to focus on moral values. I have also emphasized the importance of being silent. Silence is necessary to control the senses. Through the meditation process, you can observe your mind and focus your attention.

In this book I have discussed all those topics with His Excellency Dalai lama and he told the solution of these topics. There is a way in this book how to improve **ourselves for Good** and **achieve** our **goal in life**.

Small steps taken by us take us towards the goal of our life and **Moksha (Salvation)** is the ultimate aim of our birth on this earth.

With this ebook I have tried my best to solve your problems so that you feel happiness and achieve your Goal in life.

And I did it for you! I wish you a Great Journey in your life!!

Introduction
for happy and meaningful life

I considered myself to be a luckiest person who had eight audiences (meetings) with H.H. Dalai Lama, peace loving, great personality, and beloved by all on the earth. Once I had a desire to have an audience with this great personality and was turned into reality not only for once, but eight times. It is miracle for me.

In the first time, he sat back in his chair, with a merry twinkle in his eyes, and watched carefully to see if I had brain enough to understand the full significance of what he had said to me.

According to him, many people love me and many love my smile. Despite to my old age, my face is quite young and that is why many are friendly to me.

With every audience I spoke to him on various issues relating to our daily routine, every time I had relaxed answers which leads to change my way of living, forced me to write a book relating to existing problems in the modern world as suggested me by H.H. Dalai Lama. In the 8th audience I had an opportunity to attend one hour session of H.H. Dalai

Lama. In this session he was able to touch lot of issues and problems of the universe. This session was especially on education. He is treasure of knowledge; I also learnt a lot of things from this session. I had grasped the idea to write something, preparing myself to take it to the world, to men and women.

The Buddhist philosophy teaches that if you hate the other, you will be the first person who will be harmed.

All of us know it very well about H.H. Dalai Lama; his country was snatched away from him by the Chinese government. H.H. Dalai Lama refuses to hate the Chinese government for doing it. Why? It is a question for our new generation.

Answer is very simple.

According to Dalai Lama, if you think of hurting others, if you think negative towards others, they will be hurt later on; you will be hurt first of all.

It is the live example of the Dalai Lama being taught all over the world.

Dharamshala, at the height of 1457m (4780ft) above the sea, is surrounded by cedar forests on the edge of the Himalayas. Mcleodganj, 2082m (6831ft), is a part of Dharamshala in Distt. Kangra of Himachal Pradesh. It is also known as 'Little Lahsa', its large population is Tibetan. Mcleodganj is the capital of the Tibetan government-in-exile. Mcleoganj is the home place of 14th Dalai Lama. It is known as Tsuglagkhang (residence of Dalai Lama). Namgyal Monastery is world famous, tourists all over the world visit here throughout the year. Thekchen Choling Temple ---- complex of spiritual center for Tibetan Buddhism. It has become paradise for foreign and Indian travellers.

The Dalai Lama is considered a living Buddha of compassion, a reincarnation of the bodhisattva Chenrezig, who renounced Nirvana in order to help mankind. But starting in the 17th century, the Dalai Lama also wielded full political authority over the secretive kingdom.

The Dalai Lama, the exiled religious and political leader of Tibet, is awarded the Nobel Peace Prize in recognition of his nonviolent campaign to end the Chinese domination of Tibet. The 14th Dalai Lama was born as Tenzin Gyatso in a hamlet in northeastern Tibet in 1935.

The 14th and current Dalai Lama is Tenzin Gyatso, who lives as a refugee in India. The Dalai Lama is also considered to be the successor in a line of tulkus who are believed to be incarnations of Avalokiteśvara, the Bodhisattva of Compassion.

The Dalai Lama belongs to the Gelugpa tradition of Tibetan Buddhism, this is the largest and most influential tradition in Tibet. On April 29, 1959, the Dalai Lama established the independent Tibetan government in exile, the Central Tibetan

Administration, in the north Indian hill station of Mussoorie, which then moved in May 1960 to Dharamsala, where he resides.

When the Nobel Committee chose the Dalai Lama, it emphasized that he based his Buddhist peace philosophy on reverence for all living things and the idea of a universal responsibility that embraces both man and nature.

The Five Precepts

1. Refrain from taking life. Not killing any living being.

2. Refrain from taking what is not given. Not stealing from anyone.

3. Refrain from the misuse of the senses. Not having too much sensual pleasure.

4. Refrain from wrong speech. Not lying or gossiping about other people.

5. Refrain from intoxicants that cloud the mind.

The teachings of the Buddha are aimed solely at liberating sentient beings from suffering, because humans are sentient being. The **Basic Teachings of Buddha** which are core to Buddhism are:

1. **The Three Universal Truths**

    (a). Nothing is lost in the universe.

    (b). Everything Changes.

    (c). the Law of Cause and Effect in Buddhism,

The law of karma says "for every event that occurs there will follow another event whose existence was caused by the first, and this second event will be pleasant or unpleasant according as its cause was skillful or unskillful." Therefore, the law of Karma teaches that the responsibility for unskillful actions is borne by the person who commits them.

2. The Four Noble Truths

These may be described as:

(i). **Dukkha:** Suffering exists: Life is suffering. Suffering is real and almost universal. Suffering has many causes: loss, sickness, pain, failure, and the impermanence of pleasure.

(ii). **Samudaya**: There is a cause of suffering. Suffering is due to attachment. It is the desire to have and control things. It can take many forms: craving of sensual pleasures; the desire for fame; the desire to avoid unpleasant sensations, like fear, anger or jealousy.

(iii). **Nirodha:** There is an end to suffering. Attachment can be overcome. Suffering ceases with the final liberation of Nirvana (Nibbana). The mind experiences complete freedom, liberation and non-attachment. It lets go of any desire or craving.

(iv). **Magga:** In order to end suffering, you must follow the Eightfold Path. There is a path for accomplishing this. There is a path for accomplishing this. **The five precepts: - These are rules to live by.**

(1). **Do not kill.** This is sometimes translated as "not harming" or an absence of violence.

(2). **Do not steal.** This is generally interpreted as including the avoidance of fraud and economic exploitation.

(3). **Do not lie.** This is sometimes interpreted as including name-calling, gossip, etc.

(4). **Do not misuse sex.** For monks and nuns, this means any departure from complete celibacy. For the laity, adultery is forbidden, along with any sexual harassment or exploitation, including that within marriage.

(5). **Do not consume alcohol or other drugs.** The main concern here is that intoxicants cloud the mind. Some have included as a drug other methods of divorcing ourselves from reality -- e.g. movies, television, and the Internet. Those preparing for monastic life or who are not within a family are expected to avoid an additional five activities.

3. The Noble Eightfold Path

The Way to the End of Suffering

The Buddha's Eightfold Path consists of: Panna: Discernment, wisdom:

(1). **Samma ditthi**: Right Understanding of the Four Noble Truths. Right View is the true understanding of the four noble truths.

(2). **Samma sankappa**: Right thinking; following the right path in life. Right Aspiration is the true desire to free oneself from attachment, ignorance, and hatefulness. These two are referred to as Prajna, or Wisdom. Sila: Virtue, morality:

(3). **Samma vaca**: Right speech: No lying, criticism, condemning, gossip, harsh language. Right Speech involves abstaining from lying, gossiping, or hurtful talk.

(4). **Samma kammanta:** Right conduct or Right Action involves abstaining from hurtful behaviors, such as killing, stealing, and careless sex. These are called the Five Precepts.

(5). **Samma ajiva:** Right livelihood: Support yourself without harming others. Right Livelihood means making your living in such a way as to avoid dishonesty and hurting others, including animals. These three are referred to as Shila, or Morality. Samadhi: Concentration, meditation:

(6). **Samma vayama:** Right Effort: Promote good thoughts; conquer evil thoughts. Right Effort is a matter of exerting oneself in regards to the content of one's mind: Bad qualities should be abandoned and prevented from arising again. Good qualities should be enacted and nurtured.

(7). **Samma sati:** Right Mindfulness: Become aware of your body, mind and feelings. Right Mindfulness is the focusing of one's attention on one's body, feelings, thoughts, and consciousness in such a way as to overcome craving, hatred, and ignorance.

(8). **Samma samadhi:** Right Concentration: Meditate to achieve a higher state of consciousness. Right Concentration is meditating in such a way as to progressively realize a true understanding of imperfection, impermanence, and non-separateness. There are, however, many sects of Buddhism and there are different kinds of Buddhist monks all over the world. The life and customs of Buddhist monks are not only different and unique but consist of a spiritual meaning. Their daily life follows a strict schedule that revolves around meditation, study of scriptures, and taking part in ceremonies.

I learnt from Guru ji to always put love and compassion before judgment. Be true to yourself, be forgiving of missed deadlines and help others get in touch with their best selves. Happiest people are the ones who make others happy.

Contents

Acknowledgements .... *iii*
Preface .... *v*
Introduction for happy and meaningful life .... *viii*
Materialistic World 1
Thoughts 10
Emotions 15
Visualization and subconscious have deep
relationship between them. 28
Theory of Let-Go 34
Small Steps towards Happiness 45
Effective Communication 59
Education and Compassion 70
Moksha (Salvation) 83
Ultimate way to reach 92
Conclusion 105

Materialistic World

Our desires are never- ending. Everyone is chasing the wrong one, why it is so? He wants every comforts, everything your body needs or of having a pleasant life, the feeling of physically relaxed and in no pain; that provides you with everything your needs. They are in the opinion of something that makes your life easier and more pleasant. Do you think that you are happy?

One day I was having a talk with my colleague who is also connected with spiritualism and I asked him why the most of people are not happy. He also replied the same answer in this way. He said, "Suppose our desire is to have our own house and it is materialized. After that he will think about to have his own car, and it is materialized. Next he will think about some other luxury things and his desires will not full stop." This is reason of his unhappiness. He tries to become richer and richer.

According to Buddhist philosophy,

There are **four golden truths**:-

1. There is suffering in this world.
2. This suffering has a cause.
3. The cause of the suffering is Desire.
4. The desire is removed; then suffering is removed.

About happiness and peace, Lord Krishna has given the formula in Bhagwat Gita. He said, "How will you get peace? The answer is simple. Give up desires, you will become peaceful."

It is my conclusion that desire is the root cause of all our problems.

We all are human being, we all are same; same means emotionally, mentally and physically same. More important, every human desires to be happy life, joyful life and meaningful life; don't want strain or any problem. Everyone has the same right.

We live in a fast moving technological world with people scattered all around the globe busy with their own commitments and in turn miss the various emotions of life. Happiness is one such emotion that cannot be provided by technology. Because of New Technology, we are close to each other i.e. reality.

Man is a social animal; one brilliant mind cannot survive in alone. All continents are heavily interconnected. And they are dependent on each other.

But there are some issues-----------Environmental problems, Global economy, new modern Technology and others. In the modern technology, our youth is in stress throughout the world. He is so busy that he cannot spare a single minute for others.

Materialistic happiness is only on a sensorial level, seeing something nice, hearing some beautiful music, and taste and smell and touch including sex. Generation coming from our Education system eventually create materialistic life, materialistic culture, because our existing system of education is very much oriented about Material Education. In the whole world, even every corner of the world, every education system is creating materialistic education, materialistic culture. So people pay more attention towards materialistic values. No doubt, we should pay attention about material values; our never-ending desires demand this system. Then such person comes across some mental level problems, and then they read about happiness. But these are Materialistic happiness on a material level. If we are having too much facility, too much anger and anxiety is inside. These are short-lived, not long lasting happiness. Now the question raises how to be happy? What to do and how to live?

We must consider seven billion people as a part of us. Truly we are one community, one human family with the convention that physically, mentally and emotionally, we are same. We must share this view. Now we should raise need of sense of Global Responsibility. Take care of others and getting affection from them. For this three factors are important----------Compassion, Spirit of forgiveness and Realistic attitude.

These three things come from inner values and bring inner comforts.

Every human being has a right to be happy life. Our main purpose in life is Happiness and joyful life. What are the social forces and society role in attaining happiness? The answer is very simple. We should pay equal attention about material values as well as inner values. A balance must be maintained. Happiness is a part of our inner experience which must develop within our mind. No doubt our life is very precious. Life is like a coin, it has two sides and we are in such a point where only one side of the coin is visible, but other side which is not visible, we are ignorant because of anyone guided/suggested us. Remember this thing that other side is waiting for its turn. Now time has come we should pay more attention to our inner values.

Happiness means how we are in our inner lives----- our thoughts, emotions, beliefs and desires. A sense of inner peace both peace of mind and peace in the heart.

"Your beliefs have the power to unlock your inner genius or keep you from fully achieving your greatest potential."

Connecting with those you love, like and appreciate you restores the spirit and gives you energy to keep moving forward in this life.

"Renewal requires opening yourself up to new ways of thinking and feeling"

The best way to insure you achieve the greatest satisfaction out of life is to behave intentionally. Every goal first starts as something in our mind. You have it all within you.

I encourage you to commit to make to your life the life you want to live and embrace it.

In my opinion in regard to happiness, where we convinced, we get true happiness. There are **three truths in the Materialistic world** in our life:-

1. Money: - Some people firmly believe in money. They think that everything is money and happiness is in money. Their entire energy, their entire efforts, even their entire life is spent in the pursuit of earning money. Money is everything for them.

2. Fame: - Some people believe that happiness is in gaining fame and prestige in life. They think that fame and prestige would bring happiness. Therefore they spend all efforts and entire energy in this game.

3. In God: - Many of the people have different view, but their number is less as comparison to above mentioned categories. They believe that happiness is in God. They strive to know and love God. They are spiritual minded people. They try to connect themselves with God. They are not running after the wrong.

When we choose happiness in the wrong place that becomes the cause of our suffering and our miseries. Hence, by using our intellect, we can analyze the real position and understand where the real happiness lies that will satisfy us.

Happiness is nothing; it is merely the satiation of the desire.

Now you are at a point where desire is eliminated and you are thinking, "I am happy."

The real happiness is in God.

Try to reach Him. We can reach God on the basis of two simple ways:-

1. When we cleanse our hearts.
2. When we purify our mind.

Meaning of first line is by growing from within and meaning of second by becoming a better person from inside.

If we can understand this important point rather than running around for external enhancements. Give a priority in our life for internal growth.

Hence real happiness is experienced, by growing from within and becoming a better person from inside.

Karmic Account:

First I'll give some importance to our Karmic Account and will throw a light on this topic.

We need to settle our Karmic account. Let go means past, it will not come again. One should be clear that whatever happened was as per my Karmic account. What he/she did to me a part of the karmic, GIVE and TAKE which I had with them? It was a relationship of my earlier birth, not be ignored.

Law which is applicable to one and to all in this universe; according to this we are incarnate birth on the earth.

1. If you are performing bad action, and doing wrong. It is sure that bound to go down; no one can pull you up.

2. If you are good and doing good things, good action. Your result in back is to go you up. No one can harm you; no one can pull you down.

This is Law of Karma; this is Law of Nature

I'll try my best to explain the Theory of Karma. I'll take up the case of my subordinate. I was posted an institution where a couple (both husband and wife) was working in this institution. They were very hard working and punctual to their duties, but they always complaint of their son. They had two sons; one of them was born handicapped; he was unable to walk. They asked God, "What did they do to have this child? The other people are not like this, they are blessed with beautiful life. It seems that God is very unfair. This is gross partiality." But they are ignorant of truth and the logic behind it is not known to them. Then, I tried to find out the exact answer and truth of their dissatisfaction. I consulted many books and took the help of YOU-TUBE. One day I could find the only logical sensible answer for this. The only answer is that this is the Theory of Karma; means Karmas carried forward from past lives. Karmas that we have done not in one life in the endless past lifetimes, God is a supreme judge (keeping his eyes open) and records our all activities whether we are knowingly or unknowingly doing them. God is keeping our account in every fraction of second. As per our account, there is our account balance sheet. This balance sheet is called Sanchita Karmas. Sanchita Karma is the accumulated karma of our past lifetimes minus what we have already burned out. So every time when God sends us into the world to continue our journey. He opens our balance sheet and takes one portion from the Sanchita Karma and gives it. This portion we have to bear in the lifetime; it is called our destiny. We cannot run away from this destiny with which we are born. There is an element of destiny in everybody's life, none can deny it.

We see in life most of the people expect good outcomes even for bad Karma they have performed. But they forget that fruit depends on our actions. Therefore we must be careful about our actions in daily life and do only **Good.**

Thoughts

Every reality starts from a single dream of thought; work hard, focus on it and make consistency ----- success is definite for you. Nothing is impossible, everything is possible.

Man can create nothing which he does not first conceive in the form of an impulse of Thought. Everything which man creates begins in the form of thought impulse. Thought conceive in mind through the aid of imagination, which comes from our five senses. These thought impulses assembled into plans. The imagination may be used for the creation of plans or purposes that leads to success. All thought impulses intended for transmutation into physical reality. Man's thought impulses begin immediately to translate themselves into their reality, whether those are voluntary or involuntary.

There is one thing which we do throughout the day, we do it even we are asleep at night. There is not a moment in our lifetime when we are not doing it. And that is ---------Thinking. Thoughts never stop. Our thoughts can become fewer or excessive, but our thinking cannot completely stop. When we worried, if the mind is burdened, if some said, "We are feeling bad about something." And there is a worry about future. Then we will have more thoughts which mean the number of thoughts increases. The quality of thoughts may not be right; speed of the thoughts may be higher. At such time we overthink. It feels as if there is neither a comma nor full stop to our thoughts. Questions like why, ------what, ------how------our thoughts occur at a very fast pace, the speed of thoughts increase. On the other hand when we are peaceful, when we meditate, our thoughts decrease or reduce which means number of thoughts comes down, because the quality of every thought will be very good. When we are asleep, the first stage is when we are dreaming. During this time, the speed of thoughts will be less than the normal speed of thoughts. After that we go into a state of deep sleep for some time. In this phase the speed of thoughts will be very less. It feels as if there are no thoughts created. But there is never a movement in life when we are never creating a thought.

First of all we need to understand what the source of thought is. From where does it come to our mind? We understand this process in the following way.

Our every thought is our creation. Every thought is energy. What is the source of this thought energy? Every human being is source of Energy. Structure of our body is like this:-

Our body is made of organs. Every organ is consists of tissues and every tissue has cells, and these cells are made of Atoms.

Organs------= Tissues-------= Cells-------= Atoms

Atom (Protons, Electrons, and Neutrons) is not a solid particle, it is Energy. The science has proved it. As a result of this all of us are made of energy. Energy has vibrations. Thought is the energy. What is the raw material that creates this energy?

Information is the most important source of thoughts. It is like food we eat, food is the source of energy for the body. It also creates the immunity system of the body. It is based on our diet. Now what creates my mind? It is my diet which creates my mind. Which diet? My emotional diet, what is my emotional diet? Answer is very simple-------- INFORMATION.

Information includes everything that we see, watch and read, all these are stored in the mind. They are stored in the subconscious mind and become a part of our thoughts.

Information is the source of vibrations.

How do the vibrations produced in our body? What type of vibrations produced in our body? It depends upon Emotions. And these emotions are controlled by our belief system (may be negative or positive). Belief system is engraved inside you. The following factors are controlling our belief system:

a) A person's good and bad actions in this and previous states of existence, viewed as affecting their future -------- theory of Karma

b) Your Sacrament (Sanskars)

c) Incidents happened in your life

d) Psyche Impressions

As a result of these factors our emotions may be positive or negative. These emotions are responsible to our success or failure which leads to physical reality.

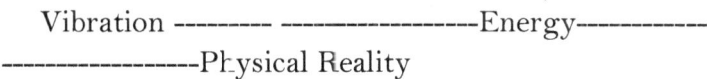

Vibration --------- ------------------Energy------------ -------------------Physical Reality

Question is that how vibration is produced? Vibration is produced by our belief system; it may be positive or negative. Belief system depends on three things: -- your past Karma, your Sacrament (Sanskars) and incidents happened in your life (Psyche impressions). Your belief system will completely change if your negativity is zero. Make it sure that negativity should be zero. For zero negativity, Kasrmic lyre should be dissolved and release your psyche impressions.

Match your vibration with your desire. Let your vibration match your desire. What is desire? What is vibration? Match your vibration with your desire means what we want in Reality. For this, simple two steps are taken or adopted: ----

First Step: Never mind what I am.

Second Step: Start imagines what I want.

So our thoughts do not depend on how the situation is. Everything depends on how our thoughts are. So we should not make our thoughts dependent on the situation. We need to change the situation using our thoughts. Because our thoughts create our world, our thoughts create our feelings. Our thoughts affect our body.

Because where is every thought from the mind reaching, you must remain positive in the mind. Program your mind to think positive always. By your positive thinking, your destiny will be changed. When you think right, you will be benefited.

In order to make your life a success, the one ability we need to master more than anything else is the ability of how to think and how not to think. First we must realize the importance of our thoughts. Thinking can make us successful and happy.

This is one of the best ways of your life to be Happy.

Emotions

Our emotional health is dependent on our emotional diet. Emotional diet means what we watch, what we read and what we listen. Plus what we eat and we drink. All five of them have their vibrations. These vibrations are the result of Emotions-----Positive and Negative.

Holding tension in our tissues is the result of energy being held and not released. This tension holds its grip along the lines of connection in our body – the meridians – and disrupts the alignment of muscle and joints. Therefore, our movement patterns don't allow the forces or load of activity to flow freely and with ease so instead our tissues become overloaded and we know that tension in our tissues is unreleased energy that wants to be in motion. It is Emotion. Tension in muscles is unreleased energy.

We talk about 'holding' our tension here or there, or wherever. We haven't let it go. Energy wants to be in motion, not stored. Energy in motion – emotion – is what wants releasing. This may seem like a quantum leap, but e-motions are e-nergy in motion.

It comes back to the name – e-motion. Energy that is to be in motion, Emotions want to flow. And the only way for emotions to flow in the first instance is to truly have a channel for releasing, or feeling our feelings. To allow them to arise and to be fully expressed, the joy, the anger, the happiness, the grief, the fear, the sadness, the excitement...

...the only way for emotions to flow is to truly have a channel for releasing, or feeling our feelings. To allow them to arise and to be fully expressed, only when fully expressed – fully felt, fully breathed into – can their inherent energy be in motion and therefore released. Fully released they can no longer have a hold on us. This is true from the perspective of being mentally tormented by them, as well as them no longer having a hold on our tissues.

The truth is that our Eastern practices have understood emotions and their connection to the body in a far greater depth than we have in the West. Eastern models understand that different emotions are held in different regions of the body and that in fact they're held by different organs. At some point here in the West our ancestors must have understood this to some extent because our language reflects this

– we experience joy in our heart, have butterflies in our stomach; we get choked up with emotion; our heart aches… Over recent years the tenets of Western biology have been catching up to these ancient Eastern understandings and establishing that from physical perspective, different emotions do have an impact on the physiology of our organs.

In effect, our emotions are a function of a chemical reaction within cells. Cells function according to the building blocks that they receive – their environment. Provide poor nutrition to our cells and they won't function well…just like putting the wrong fuel into the car. And say you live your life constantly worried – anxious or in fear – this will have a physical counterproductive effect on the flow of essential chemical reactions within the cells of your body as well.

If our cells have not released their grip on us, there will be a disturbance along the chain in relation to the muscle and soft tissue, but their equivalent, internal version. It is in this way that from their internal to external connections, that emotional tension we are holding onto internally can have an external effect on our physical musculoskeletal system. From this perspective, physical pain stems from emotional pain… Suppress emotion and it will find its way to the physical body.

I happen to think that at the base of all pain is emotional pain. That is unreleased emotions. In truth, we've probably all had experience of this...we've been heartbroken and experienced the physical wrench it has on our body and on our inability to function optimally. We understand how the depth of grief too can debilitate us, and how this will literally stop us in our physical tracks. On a positive note, though – we've also all felt the physical lift of joy and laughter, the well-being of love.

These are all heart-based emotions, and all of these feelings have to be fully experienced in order for us to resume normal function once again...for us to find balance once again. This is also why we say that we've had a 'visceral reaction' to an event, or seeing some distressing documentary for example – literally, the organs (the viscera) experienced the emotion! Our emotions show themselves for a purpose – to be experienced, or 'felt', to get our attention and either to make us feel good or to make us feel not so good. They are there for their message to be understood, to help guide us – literally towards the 'good' and away from the 'bad'.

So when we fully experience our emotions and take heed of their message, they no longer have to have a grip on us, in any sense. Where our pain arises in our body is not random. In addition, it's not altogether simply a function of having had 'an injury', an accident or mishap either. These things show themselves in our physical body when the body is trying to get our attention over some other matter.

Oftentimes an injury is literally making us to stop and listen, to take heed of what its saying. Our yoga practice encourages us to be gentle with ourselves. Our meditation is a space to allow the thoughts and the feelings to rise – to allow them – and then to let them go. Be aware of their presence; to acknowledge them, and then remove them from any attachment to us. Clearly, this is sometimes easier said than done...but seeking help, well, helps! It is, however, essential so that our emotions cannot have a hold on us, allow them to dissipate and thus allowing, physically, flowing them.

It is well-known fact that emotion rules the majority of people. The subconscious mind responds more quickly to, and is influenced more readily by thought impulses which are well mixed with emotion, it is essential to become familiar with types of emotions.

There are many different types of emotions that have an influence on how we live and interact with others. At times, it may seem like we are ruled by these emotions. The choices we make, the actions we take, and the perceptions we have are all influenced by the emotions we are experiencing at any given moment.

There are four kinds of basic emotions: happiness, sadness, fear, and anger, which are differentially associated with three core affects: reward (happiness), punishment (sadness), and stress (fear and anger).

There are some other emotions, but I am not discussing them.

After conceiving the thought in your mind and your mind is ready or prepared to receive it, there are three enemies will come to your way of journey. These three are Indecision, Doubt and Fear. These are negative emotions. Any one of them remains in your mind, where one is found, the other two are close at hand. Indecision is the seeding of Fear. Indecision crystalized into Doubt, the two blends and becomes Fear.

This is one reason why these three enemies are so dangerous for any positive growth in life.

Negative Emotion

1. Self-Centered Attitude (I, My, Myself)

2. We do not accept reality as appears, nothing exists as it appear.

These are two factors are the basis of negative emotions. Negative thoughts and emotions undermine the very causes of peace and happiness. In fact, when we think properly, it is totally illogical to seek happiness if we do nothing to restrain angry, spiteful and malicious thoughts and emotions.

H.H. Dalai Lama believes that 'Just as we teach about physical hygiene in the interest of good health, we now need to teach about emotional hygiene.'

Obviously anger, hatred and fear are destructive emotions. Anger is the most dangerous in health point of view. These emotions destroy our inner peace. Constructive emotions like Compassion (Karuna) and Patience, these are emotions of the antidotes to these destructive emotions. So, like physical health, good health will not be achieved through prayer, but you take the care of your body and avoid some germs and other negative things, then the immune system will increase. Similarly, for mental level we should identify what kind of emotion is the antidote to destructive emotions. That is the way of training our mind. In education, from the Kindergarten level we usually include education about physical hygiene. Now the time has come to include hygiene of emotions that is very important. Train your mind to see the good in everything. Positivity is a choice. The happiness of your life depends on the quality of your thoughts.

Here is one question——

Should we include the chapter of hygiene of emotions in our educational system? Answer is yes.

It is great necessity to teach this education in every stage of the education system. Just as we teach about physical hygiene in the interest of good health, we now need to teach about mental or emotional hygiene too. We need to observe emotional hygiene to preserve a healthy mind and attitude. People may hear your words, but they feel your attitude. Your problem is not the problem; it is your attitude about the problem.

Ability is what you are capable of doing. Motivation determines what you do. Attitude determines how well you do it.

There are some other negative emotions, I'll not mention them.

Positive emotions are magnetic forces through which we can achieve any goal in life. Thought which are mixed with any of the positive emotions constitute a magnetic force which attracts from the vibrations of ether, other similar or related thoughts. A thought thus magnetized with emotion is a seed which planted in fertile soil, germinates, grows and multiplies itself over and over again until that which was originally one small seed becomes countless millions of seeds.

Positive and Negative emotions cannot occupy the mind at the same time. One or the other must dominate. It is your responsibility to make sure that positive emotions constitute the dominating influence of your mind. Here the law of habit will come to your aid. From the habit of applying and using the positive emotions! Eventually, they will dominate your mind so completely that the negative emotions cannot enter it. The presence of a single negative in your conscious mind is sufficient to destroy all chances of constructive growth.

By thinking again and again on a particular subject, contemplation again and again your mental habits are developed. These mental habits are responsible for growth or fall, success or failure. They can pull us down or they can lift us up. Therefore we must be careful about our contemplation; we must realize the importance of contemplation.

These negative emotions can be handling by contemplation on the positive things. Take the help of the scriptures for gaining knowledge. For take the case of anger. Anger is a bad thing. I must never become angry, thinking again and again. It is hurtful and harmful. You contemplate over this again and again, do some mental practice. In this way the situation will change. Your behavior, your inter relationship, everything will be transformed. Lack of knowledge we are away from happiness. Why don't we benefit from them? Lack of contemplation! Pick one piece of wisdom and contemplate over it. In this way you have developed a handle over your emotions. Continue the process, one day you will reach a particular point where you have become free of the environment, where it doesn't matter how difficult the environment, you realize that your thoughts and your emotions are your own choice.

Rather choosing externals, you can choose to be positive, to be hopeful, to be devoted and to be virtuous.

Concentrate yourself on the following beautiful lines

Your mind is a garden; your thoughts are seeds, you can grow flowers, or you can grow weeds.

Subconscious Mind and Visualization

The subconscious mind is consist of a field of consciousness in which every impulse of thought that reaches the objective mind through any of the five senses, classified and recorded. It receives and files of sense impressions or thoughts. You may voluntarily plan in your subconscious mind any plan which you desire to translate into physical reality. How it works. We understand in the following way.

Man creates thoughts. On what basis are our thoughts created?

When there is a stimulus in front of us, in response to this we create a thought. We are independent to make a choice of thought. When we something or the scene through our sense organs; we take that information in, because information is the source of thought. Where does information come to you? Simple answer is through sense organs, also from past experience and belief system. These are the sources of thoughts.

When information came in through sense organs, we created a thought in response to that information. Not a single thought, many thoughts are created. These thoughts got stored in our memory and everything gets recorded in the mind. Then these thoughts are analyzed and evaluated by intellect. It is the duty of intellect to take decision. Whenever intellect took the decision, we brought it into Action. Once the brain cells receive the message, and the Karma (action) was created through body. Next time the same information came in and same thought created. Now what would be the role intellect? Same order was given to body and body did the same Karma again. In this way whole process is repeated multiple times. Now understand the role of conscious mind and subconscious mind. It has gone into subconscious mind from the conscious mind. Subconscious mind is a lyre, of which we are not aware throughout the day.

According to Freud, the unconscious mind is the primary source of human behavior. Like an iceberg, the most important part of the mind is the part you cannot see. Our feelings, motives and decisions are actually powerfully influenced by our past experiences, and stored in the unconscious.'

The Iceberg Metaphor

Freud often used the metaphor of an iceberg to describe the two major aspects of human personality. The tip of the iceberg that extends above the water represents the conscious mind. As you can see in the image on top, the conscious mind is just the "tip of the iceberg." Beneath the water is the much larger bulk of the iceberg, which represents the unconscious.

While the conscious and subconscious are important, Freud believed that they were far less vital than the subconscious. The things that are hidden from awareness, Freud believed, exerted the greatest influence over our personalities and behaviors.

When conceptualizing the subconscious mind, it can be helpful to compare the mind to an iceberg. Everything above the water represents conscious awareness while everything below the water represents the subconscious.

Consider how an iceberg would look if you could see it in its entirety. Only a small part of the iceberg is actually visible above the water. What you cannot see from the surface is the enormous amount of ice that makes up the bulk of the iceberg, submerged deep below in the water.

The things that represent our conscious awareness are simply "the tip of the iceberg." The rest of the information that is outside of conscious awareness lies below the surface. While this information might not be accessible consciously, it still exerts an influence over current behavior.

How much of an Iceberg is really visible to us? We see only 10%, this part is visible to us and to the world. It is known as Conscious mind. More than

90% is hidden below which is not visible to us; it is known as subconscious mind. Everything is being recorded in the subconscious mind. We watch, listen, think and feel, all these have recorded in the subconscious mind. How many recordings in an hour, in a day, in a lifetime, in multiple lifetimes? All this constitutes the 90% of the Iceberg which is not visible. We all are not aware of what this 90% has.

Impact of the Unconscious

Unconscious thoughts, beliefs, and feelings can potentially cause a number of problems including:

Anger

Bias

Compulsive behaviors

Difficult social interactions

Distress

Relationship problems

Freud believed that many of our feelings, desires, and emotions are repressed or held out of awareness because they are simply too threatening. Freud believed that sometimes these hidden desires and wishes make themselves known through dreams and slips of the tongue. Our natural instincts are also contained in subconscious mind.

Visualization and subconscious have deep relationship between them.

If you take a look around, you will see nothing human-made that did not first exist as an image in someone's mind. It is impossible to create something that cannot first be imagined.

To accomplish our goal faster-----------it is to tap into the power of visualization. The power of visualization is much more useful than merely writing and remembering our goals.

Some high achievers what seems like super-powers, helping them create their dream lives by accomplishing one goal or task at a time with confidence. In fact, we all are unaware of this awesome power, because most of us have never been taught to use it effectively. All Elite use it. The super-rich use it. And peak performers in all fields now use it. This power is called visualization. The daily practice of visualizing your dreams as already complete can rapidly accelerate your achievement of those dreams, goals, and ambitions.

Visualization – seeing the goal as already complete in your mind's eye – is a core technique used by the world's most successful people. Visualization is effective because it harnesses the power of our subconscious mind.

Create Goal Pictures

Another powerful visualization technique is to create a photograph or picture of yourself with your goal, as if it were already completed. If one of your goals is to become a bureaucrat, take your camera down to your District Magistrate's office and have a picture taken of yourself sitting with him of your dream. If your goal is to visit U.S.A., find a picture or poster of the statue of Liberty and cut out a picture of yourself and place it into the picture.

One more interesting and inspiring story of college life, my friend senior to me by one year, was a staying in the college hostel. He had a dream to join army as officer, so he fixed a name plate outside his room, plate showing the name Capt. Prakram Singh. He was not a brilliant student, just average. In the final year he had a supply (compartment), but his daily practice of visualizing his dream, as if he were the Captain of his platoon. That visualization went straight to the subconscious mind which is the tool of success. Eventually he was succeeded in his goal. He joined army and now he retired from army as Brigadier.

Another story of one Russian Jew named Natan Sharansky was living in communist Russia, and was accused of being an American spy. He was thrown into jail. He staged in jail for twelve years. The condition of jail was very, very bad. His body started deteriorating lack of facilities. His brain also started deteriorating. What to do for the brain? A thought was created in his mind, because as a child he was fond of chess. So he decided to play chess in his mind. Now the question was with whom to play? So he decided why not to play with the world champion. Gary Kasparov was the world champion in those days. So he used to play with Gary Kasparov in the mind. This process remained for twelve years. When Bill Clinton became the president of U.S.A. and he made an appeal to the Government of Russia. On his appeal Natan Sharansky was released from the jail. Then he decided to live in Israel, country of Jew. He went to Israel where he became a cabinet minister. One day Gary Kasparov came on a visit to Israel for demonstration matches. In the demonstration match, Gary Kasparov was playing against five players, means one against five. He defeated four of them, but he was lost to one person. Now you want to know the person whom he was defeated. He was Natan Sharansky. The people asked him, "Sir, how did you defeat the world champion? You are not a grand master of this game." His reply was this. He said, "You know, for 12 multiply by 365 means 4380 days I was defeating him every day in my mind. So I had got programmed to defeat him was the most natural thing for me. He had visualized it again and again. He had programmed his subconscious for defeating him. This was the power of visualization.

One inspiration example of my neighborhoods, one middle-aged lady was suffering from Cancer, went to MH, Yol (Himachal Pradesh) and went under treatment. A few days later she was advised to take rest at home; because it is not curable, no need to come here again. She got angry and told senior doctor she would come here after curing this disease. She didn't lose her heart. One day she was travelling in the train, an unknown person could come to her contact. He had a long talk with her and narrated her story in detail regarding her illness. After this conversation, she had a turn in her life. She started thinking positive and had an impression in her mind that she is all right; no disease. This thinking leads her to cure her disease. Within a short period, she could able to defeat her disease. This is the power of visualization.

Use Affirmations to Support Your Visualization

An affirmation is a statement that evokes not only a picture, but the experience of already having what you want. Here's an example of an affirmation:

I am happily vacationing one month out of the year in a tropical paradise, and working just four days a week owning my own business. Repeating an affirmation several times a day keeps you focused on your goal, strengthens your motivation, and programs your subconscious by sending an order to do whatever it takes to make that goal happen.

Through writing down your goals, using the power of visualization and repeating your daily affirmations, you can achieve amazing results.

Visualization and affirmations allow you to change your beliefs, assumptions, and opinions about the most important person in your life — YOU! They allow you to harness the 18 billion brain cells in your brain and get them all working in a singular and purposeful direction.

Your subconscious will become engaged in a process that transforms you forever. The process is invisible and doesn't take a long time. It just happens over time, as long as you put in the time to visualize and affirm, practice your techniques, surround yourself with positive people, read uplifting books and listen to audio programs that flood your mind with positive, life-affirming messages.

Start by picking a time during which you'll review your goals and visualize your success. Ideally, do this twice a day – first thing in the morning and right before you go to bed. The process will take less than 10 minutes.

Our goal is to purify the mind. Now, how do we this? You purify the mind by attaching it to the all pure God. To purify your mind and subconscious, you want to make them divine. You visualize the image of your God, of your Lord. To do that, you should meditate on the image of God, who is all pure and divine. Action them; think about a goal you want to achieve in your life. Make it a habit to visualize yourself in the state where you accomplished your goal. Do this the first thing in the morning after you wake up and every night before you go to sleep. You will find yourself much more inspired to work on your goal and it will result in the faster achievement.

This is tool of your achievement by attaching yourself with God in three words: Ask, Believe and Receive.

Visualization and Subconscious mind is a partner of your success.

Chapter 5

Theory of Let-Go

"Most of our troubles are due to our passionate desire for and attachment to things that we misapprehend as enduring entities."

~Dalai Lama

Beautiful things can grow when you are willing to let go.

Nothing is permanent; it is just for the fixed period, after that it will go. Then the question is that why we are holding it. When we talk of someone criticized me and I cannot forget it. Time will come I teach him a lesson and he started wasting his energy for this belief. He will not come out of it unless or until he would have a time to take the chance of this revenge. What will be the result? Is it the end point of this? No, it will add some more and ultimately they will not come near to each other.

Let it go, man!

We hear it all the time, don't we? Everyone we know wants us to let it go. But it seems impossible to the person holding on. So, what does it mean to let go?

Well, in order to answer that question we are first going to have to understand why it is that we hold on in the first place. Generally speaking, we tend to believe that the reason we hold on is because of what someone did, or didn't do, because of the loss of someone. We think that we hold on because of the circumstance—in other words, we think that we hold on because we have to change the circumstance. This belief, faulty though it is, comes from a specific stage of adjustment called "bargaining."

Now I tell you a very inspiring story of let-go. When we all are in childhood period, this theory of let-go was applied by all of us on the advice of our elders. But when we are in the age group of adult or above, we forget it. I remembered my childhood days when we are in the playing group of children (children of our brothers and sisters; children from locality) start quarrelling, even fighting. At this moment my grandmother appeared and pacified us. She said, "Raat biti, Baat biti." Means we should attached with incident which happened with. Let it go. Be friend again, otherwise it will deplete your energy regularly unless you leave it. Resentment and unwillingness to forgive will keep you locked in the past and prevent you from moving forward with your life. Again we start playing together. That time I could not understand importance of this precious advice. With the course of time I am able to understand it.

Human being that begins with our past, moves briefly through our present, and heads toward our future. Letting go of our own past—or the past we have created in our heads—can feel shaky and "ungrounded," like a boat that has slipped its mooring.

Don't try to turn it into yesterday; that moment's gone. Don't plot about how you can make the moment last forever. Just seep into the moment and enjoy it, because it will eventually pass.

It's true—tomorrow may not look the same as today, no matter how much you try to control it. A relationship might end. You might have to move. You'll deal with those moments when they come. All you need right now is to appreciate and enjoy what you have. It's enough. Nothing is permanent. Fighting that reality will only because you pain.

How many times, in our life we are not free about the things that have happened in the past. We all go through experience of guilt, regret, anger, frustration or any negative emotion in our life; we carry on those hurts and resentments in our mind. But we forget that we cannot change the past; no matter how long we carry on those thoughts in our mind. It will only cause us grief and suffering. Drop your all the emotional baggage of that event in the past and move on. Similarly we can cure this suffering by choosing to let go of what happened in the past and concentrate on the present moment.

After studying mindfulness and Buddhist philosophy, I realized that the main cause of my suffering was my inability to let go of what I can't control.

Let go applies to a lot of things that we have held onto, here on our mind. They are so old; maybe we don't even remember them well. The more matter we hold on to, the soul will be heavy. If we want remain light, happy and powerful always, and then we need to clean everything from the mind.

So, power to let go means keep our life compact and not scattered. Practice of power to let go make a habit in your life. To make a habit of this theory is not easy; it is a hard and difficult.

There will never be a time when life is simple and as per your wish. There will always be time to practice accepting the things. Every moment in your life is a chance to let go and feel peaceful. How do you let go of past hurts and move on? Holding on to the past can be a conscious decision just like letting go and moving forward can be a conscious decision.

"If you let go a little, you will have a little peace. If you let go a lot, you will have a lot of peace."

~Ajahn Chah

Here are some ways to get started and move on:

1. **Learn New:**

While denying the hurtful offence may be the first thing you may want to do, it is best to admit that it happened. Reflect upon it; take note how you reacted, and what it has done to your health and well-being. Be able to articulate what was unacceptable about the situation.

Learn something new. To think or talk a lot about something that it would be better to forget. Don't dwell on the past, let's think about the future.

2. **Create a positive mantra to counter the painful thoughts**

For example, instead of getting stuck in, "I can't believe this happened to me!" try a positive mantra such as, "I am fortunate to be able to find a new path in my life — one that is good for me."

Having this mantra that you tell yourself in times of emotional pain can help you reframe your thoughts.

3. **Keep physical distance**

Keeping physical or psychological distance between ourselves and the person or situation can help with letting go for the simple reason that we do not have to think about it, process it, or being reminded of it.

4. Focus on your own work

Focusing on you is important. When you think about a person who caused you pain, bring yourself back to the present. Then, focus on something that you're grateful for.

5. Mindfulness is important

The more we can bring our focus to the present moment and practice mindfulness. When we start practicing being present, our hurts have less control over us, and we have more freedom to choose how we want to respond to our lives.

6. Be kindness with yourself

If your first response to not being able to let go of a painful situation is to criticize yourself, it's time to show yourself some kindness and compassion. Treat ourselves like we would treat a friend, offering ourselves self-compassion, and avoiding comparisons between our journey and those of others.

Hurt is inevitable, and we may not be able to able to avoid pain; however, we can choose to treat ourselves kindly and lovingly when it comes.

7. No place for negative emotions

If you're fear of feeling negative emotions is causing you to avoid them, don't worry, you're not alone. In real life, many times, people are afraid of feelings such as grief, anger, disappointment, or sadness.

Negative emotions are like riptides. Let them flow out of you. It may require mental health intervention, but fighting them can leave you stuck.

8. Accept the person who hurt you

Waiting for an apology from the person who hurt you will slow down the process of letting go. If you're experiencing hurt and pain, it's important you take care of your own healing, which may mean accepting that the person who hurt you isn't going to apologize.

9. Give importance to self-care

When we are hurting, it often feels like there is nothing but hurt. Practice self-care can look like setting boundaries, saying no, doing the things that bring us joy and comfort, and listening to our own needs first.

Remember this important line. The more we implement self-care into our daily lives, the more empowered we are.

10. Take the help of those people who support you

We can't expect ourselves to get through our hurts alone, and we can't move on in life alone. Allowing ourselves to lean on loved ones and their support is such a wonderful way of not only limiting isolation but of reminding us of the good that is in our lives.

This is a powerful tip which helps you in strengthening your willpower.

11. Don't hesitate to talk about it

In fact, sometimes people can't let go because they feel they aren't allowed to talk.

When you're dealing with painful feelings or a situation that hurt you, it's important to give yourself permission to talk about it.

This may be because the people around them no longer want to either hear about it or embarrassed to keep talking about it. Always be agreeing without a moment's hesitation.

Hence talking it out is very important to let go.

12. Forgive to all

Make the attempt to understand the other person. Was the offense deliberate? Perhaps the person had no idea to hurt you, or was suffering from something themselves. Were there other unknown circumstances at play? Perhaps you were having a bad day; perhaps they were.

If you happen to know the hurtful act was deliberate and intended to harm you, then you may have to 'reframe' the situation. Reframing is a technique whereby you change the conceptual or emotional viewpoint from which you experience an event and put it in a different context or frame of reference. Your ability to sort through a hurtful occurrence and put it into a different framework will prepare you to begin the process of forgiveness and letting it go.

Forgiveness is a beautiful gift. Waiting for the other person to apologize can slow down the process of letting go; you have to work on your own forgiveness.

Forgiveness is vital to the healing process because it allows you to let go of anger, guilt, shame, sadness, or any other feeling you may be experiencing and move on.

13. Take the help of renowned persons

There are many renowned persons around you, if you're struggling to let go of a painful experience, you may benefit from talking to these persons. Sometimes it's difficult to implement the tips on your own, and you need experienced persons to help guide you through the process.

In my conclusion, while there is no question that we have the right to feel resentment and the desire to respond accordingly, we have the ability to make the choice not to. When we do, we refuse to play the role of the victim and we let go of the control and power that the offending person, or situation, has over us. We choose to not allow grudges, hurt or wrongdoings to define our lives.

If you commit to putting your energies on focusing on the benefits of forgiveness and letting go, you can more easily move forward with your life. With a combination of accepting, but not denying; living in the present and looking forward to the future without regret for the past, and a willingness to let go and move on will give you a gift of happy and peaceful life.

It is my humble option to all.

Let's talk about the Benefits of Forgiveness and Letting Go

1. Your happiness will increase and with the increase of happiness, your health with improved functioning of cardiovascular and nervous systems and less overall illnesses in your life. You will enjoy good health.

2. Positive thoughts and feelings will store in your mind. As a result of this, your behaviour promotes overall psychological well-being.

3. Compassion will become a part of your life style. Power of understanding the needy person will increase and healing them.

4. You will reduce stress, anxiety, depression and chronic pain

5. This will lower risk of alcohol and substance abuse

6. In every platform, your ability to function better in career, education, work place will increase.

7. You will increases hope and optimism for the future. This is a ray of light to do best in life.
8. In last, a very important benefit is relationship. In this way no enemy is in your contact and everyone will come to you when you are in need of them. Everyone will be your friend. Relation shine by shaking hands in the best moments but they blossom by holding hands in critical moments!

Counsel yourself and explain the way you do it with others. Let go, forget it, the matter is so old, put a full stop.

Now the question is, how?

How will put a full stop?

Answer is very simple, only and only way is Meditation. Meditation helps us to let-go easily. As the soul keeps filling itself with God's power, a situation which earlier seemed huge; it will now appear in significant. Once you start letting go. Our behavior will become independent of how others behave with us. You will so much inner power that even if somebody has been extremely unfair or wrong with you. You will have so much power that in one moment, you will leave it in the past. And that person is willing to make a new beginning in the relationship. You will not take time to do agree. Nevertheless you have already put a full stop to that matter; **because I am a powerful soul.**

Chapter 6

Small Steps towards Happiness

If you wait for happiness, you will wait forever.

But if you start believing that you are happy, you will be happy forever.

This is law of Nature for Life.

The Happiness of your life depends upon the quality of your thoughts.

Life teaches us a new lesson in every step, it does not mean of teaching; but it gives the message to change your thinking.

So Think positive and be happy.

"Most folks are as happy as they make up their minds to be." -- Abraham Lincoln

"Happiness is a choice, not a result. Nothing will make you happy until you choose to be happy. No person will make you happy unless you decide to be happy. Your happiness will not come to you. It can only come from you" as said by Ralph Marston.

We live in a fast moving technological world with people scattered all around the globe busy with their own commitments and in turn miss the various emotions of life. Happiness is one such emotion that cannot be provided by technology.

Our main purpose in life is Happiness, joyful and meaningful life. What are the social forces and what is the role of society in attaining the Happiness?

Very simple answer:

Every small step towards happiness is a very-very big achievement.

Many problems which we are facing are human created problems. Human made problems. Means these problems are our own creation.

Unfortunately we do not have applications/devices that can bring a smile on the people's face and give a feeling of relaxation after seeing the smile on the faces of their loved ones, the inner satisfaction that comes out without any calculation of profit or loss, or rather apps that help us to calculate how many good deeds a day we do.

Happiness is not a fruit of a tree that can be plucked by paltering stones nor is it sealed and wrapped with an expiry date nor available in any market at certain price. Like every other thing in the universe we need to put in certain extra efforts to achieve happiness. It is the pot of gold at the end of the rainbow, but the path to reach it must be carved out by one's own self. The path definitely is not going to be a bed of roses rather a bed of thorns but yet we should have the strength and courage to overcome every thorn and reach to our goal. Every path of an individual will definitely give certain lessons and experiences which if followed will lead us to the ultimate realization of life.

There are always solutions to various problems henceforth there are means to achieve happiness as well. Some of which includes doing a good deed a day.

It might be anything like helping the poor and the needy,

Spending an entire day in any orphanage or old-age home and trying to see the lives of the people staying there

Helping the physically handicapped people to overcome their challenges and have a normal life.

Helping people in and around us with a motive of pleasure and contentment not with the motive of materialistic gains

The only secret to achieve happiness is to be happy in someone else's happiness. A mother and a child relation best describe the above statement. A mother sacrifices her entire life in bringing up her child; she can do anything to bring a smile on her child's face. That smile gives her inner happiness that cannot be expressed it can only be felt.

The most important thing that requires a mention here is "Career or Work" that everyone wants the best along with its pleasures, for having the basic amenities of life, which is very important in life. Otherwise we cannot happiness in our life because if one has to think every day of earning one square meal a day then happiness will definitely have to take a back seat and remain in the clutches of what is commonly termed as "food, cloth and shelter".

Work definitely gives out an amount to carry forward with our days in the form of cheques but above these cheques also we have certain factors that need to be considered that is jobs involving adventure, challenges, and experiences and providing a wider scope of learning definitely delights a person from within and boosts oneself with confidence, faith and belief. This kind of work provides happiness rather than the old mechanized form of work that creates a certain sense of boredom among individuals. Thus happiness is one such emotion that does not requires expression rather requires feelings for its realization.

In regard of happiness, I'll quote an example of Gandhi's personal secretary named V. Kalyanam. How did he prefer to choose Ashram's life for his happiness?

He studied in Sri Ram College, Delhi and did his B.Com (Hons) in 1941. He chose to serve Gandhi Ashram in Sevagram at Wardha in 1943, when he was a young lad of 22 years instead of Government job. He didn't enjoy the Government desk job of a Budget Assistant which gave him a salary of Rs 250 per month then, which in these was certainly a princely amount. When Gandhi ji said he could not pay more than Rs 60 a month. He replied that he loved Ashram's life so much he would happily work for free and for his happiness.

The future, even this afternoon, what will happen, we don't know and for future there is no guarantee, but our life is based upon on 'Hope'. Even at present if there are difficulties, still with hope our life remains. If someone completely loses hope, then that very mental attitude shortens their life. So we conclude that hope means something good and better things for future. The purpose of our life is happiness and happiness is the real meaning of our life. That is our goal of life.

Materialistic happiness is only sensorial level, seeing something nice, hearing some beautiful music, and taste and smell. These are materialistic happiness on a material level. These are short-lived, not long lasting happiness. Long lasting happiness must develop on a mental level. In our country (India), there are many philosophies. There is no creator rather than self-creation. So there is the concept of Karma, every action you take. Everything depends on your own action. Positive action will make every human being virtuous. So in our country, for more than over 3000 years, it has been already examined, the ultimate source of happiness is not external, but internal. Not on a sensorial level, but on a mental level.

Your life is very precious. Life is like a coin— Pleasure and Pain are its two sides. Only one side is visible at a time, but remembers that other side is waiting for its turn. It is up to you take the decision. Your reaction to a situation literally has the power to change the situation itself.

Inner strength means self-confidence. When we say nice, our motivation is not very sincere, and then self-confidence is less. When motivation is very sincere, we can develop self-confidence very well. With this self-confidence your will-power increases in multiple. With will-power you can carry your life with transparency. With will-power fear reduces. Without fear, happiness comes and that is the peace of mind. This is the key factor of peace of mind.

Some of my own experiences which I learnt a lot want to share with you.

Happiness has various descriptions and meanings. Some equate it with materialistic pleasures and enjoyment and some find happiness in peace and serenity and many more. I believe it to be the ultimate realization of life.

Combining each and every aspect of happiness it can be equated with two words **"pleasure" and "contentment"**.

Activities that please human beings and give them the feeling of self- satisfaction can truly help human beings to realize happiness.

We live in a fast moving technological world with people scattered all around the globe busy with their own commitments and in turn miss the various emotions of life. Happiness is one such emotion that cannot be provided by technology.

Last year I was constructing my house I see a poor day laborer who earns his daily bread by the sweat of his brow; scarcity and poverty surround him; his entire life appears to be eternal worry, work, and want. Contentment shines from his eyes, a smile of joy graces his face, and cheerfulness and blissful oblivion surround his entire appearance. I always see him with smiling face. One day I asked him, "What do always keep you with smiling face?" For some time he did not respond. Again I asked him to reply. His reply was very simple, but valuable. He said, "My desires are zero and I never thought of future. What I earn is sufficient for my family, in this way I am always happy."

Self-satisfaction and contentment brings Happiness.

Once we visit to prisoners and have a talk with them, try to find out the reason which brought them here. You would surprise to know that a mistake which happened within a fraction of second due to negative emotion (anger). This situation may be diverted if someone has guided or educated. I'll share my experience to have a talk with such persons. A middle aged person was running a canteen outside the school. When I enquired his whereabouts, he was prisoner and completing his tenure of punishment. When I asked him what the actual cause of this incidence was. With tears in his eyes he replied it was all due to anger (negative emotion). All happened within a second. My wife brought me food and we quarreled over the taste of food. I got angry and started beating her; I was out of my control. She fell down on the ground; never stood up and could not survive.

Same incidence was occurred in a village near to Rehan in Himachal Pradesh. The only son of teacher-couple (both husband & wife were teachers) was murdered by the neighbor. He was playing with other children in the courtyard of his neighbor. This was his fault objected by the neighbor. This is not fault, children can play (time period of playing is short, not a long duration).

Kill these negative emotions, hundred percent Happiness in our hands.

There are always solutions to various problems henceforth there are means to achieve happiness as well. Some of which include doing a good deed a day,

It might be anything like helping the poor and the needy, (this is compassion). When we help a needy person, we feel automatically happiness. This is true happiness.

I went to a medical store to purchase some daily requirement, I saw an old-aged man was sitting outside the shop; he was again and again requesting shopkeeper in symbols. I asked the old man. He narrated his story that his relative in hospital and doctor asked me to bring medicines, but I had some short of money and requested the shopkeeper to pay the balance within two or three days. He did not consider my request. Then I did my duty and saw a beautiful smile on his face. It brings happiness for me.

The whole world is in the grip of Corona, many of us are in immediate help of others for their survival. Many have lost their jobs; others have no work, their earnings are almost zero. During this pandemic hour, we can share our earnings with them by donating as per our pocket. This is seed of compassion which brings you happiness.

Spending an entire day in any orphanage or old-age home and trying to see the lives of the people staying there.

I have seen many people visiting and helping the children of slum areas. I have had an opportunity to spend some time with children of slum; an interaction with them, teaching them and valuable suggestions given by them.

By the grace of God, once in my job career I had a chance to serve in physically handicapped children institution. It was day boarding school and I was head of this institution. I'll not mention what I did for them, but I put my best efforts in the welfare of these children which provides me happiness. I'll remember this tenure throughout whole life.

Helping the physically handicapped people to overcome their challenges and have a normal life.

I served the institution where two persons of this category were working there, one of them was a female; her position was more critical. She could not do anything without a helper. I decided to help her to overcome her challenges. Being head of the institution, I gave due respect to all staff members and their suggestions are always welcomed for the development and smooth running of the institution. I also took the suggestions of these two physically handicapped persons and made their participation in every activity. I gave them the task of responsibility and encouraged them in every step which was not earlier done with them.

Help people in and around us with a motive of pleasure and contentment not with the motive of materialistic gains.

The only secret to achieve happiness is to be happy in someone else's happiness. A mother and a child relation best describe the above statement. A mother sacrifices her entire life in bringing up her child; she can do anything to bring a smile on her child's face. That smile gives her inner happiness that cannot be expressed it can only be felt.

The other way to achieve happiness is to do a noble cause to think about Environment; save the earth for generation. One of the simplest ways to celebrate your birthday by planting new plants (minimum five plants) on your birthday is the best way. This formula was given to me from my son. On the day of his seventh birthday, he refused celebrating his birthday with cake party; he has decided to celebrate the occasion with different way by planting of new plants. This idea was germinated in his mind by his school teachers. It has been become his habit forever. This helps in realization of Happiness. The future of coming generation entirely depends upon our activities. Small steps can save their future by our determination in the positive direction.

In our daily there are so many little steps where we can find Happiness. Happiness is the state of mind,

mind set up which we give the direction in the positive or negative side. Positive side is the realization of happiness. It may be clear by this example.

I asked a question from a young lady who (she) is Doctor. When you come to home after finishing your duties; what happens with you. She replied, "After having a cup of tea served by my mother-in-law, same routine of work begins to starts----prepare food for dinner, look after children, and daily routine work. No rest."

I asked the same question from her mother-in-law. She replied that whole of the day I worked continuously without taking any rest when her son and daughter-in-law happily used to go for their duties.

In both cases the situation may be transformed to a constructive and positive direction if both take their daily home work/task as their own duty in welfare of family and maintaining peace and peaceful atmosphere in their family. It is their own family and no out-sider will come in their family matters. Consider it as part of their duty in welfare of their family. Make up their minds to be happy.

A beautiful message from a song film 'Anari' posturized on a popular hero RajKapoor and playback singer Mr. Mukesh and song 'Kisi ki Muskurahaton Pe Ho Nisar, Kisi Ka Dard mil sake Toh Le Udhar, Kisi Ke Vaste Ho Tere Dil Me Pyar; Jina Isi Ka Naam

Hey. (If you can get someone's pain, if you can get someone's smile, take a loan, for someone's sake, there is love in your heart; this is called the living.)

When I was in job, those moments were very happy for me when the little children of Primary School used to come to me and said that come to our class and teach us. I never discouraged them and always I turned to their class for their happiness. Even though, it was not a part of my official duty. My official duty was to teach senior secondary classes. I did not get as much as happiness other than that. Teaching is my passion and hobby. Even now, I take time out to visit the children of the slum and teach them. There is no happiness anywhere else than this and this is the way to happiness for me.

I **conclude** with the following few lines, these are very important to be Happy in life.

When we think right, we will anyway benefit, but direct effect happens to the people about whom we are thinking. So however far away you are from your family. Just like you are physically strong, likewise you need to be emotionally strong and think right for them. Only and only right thoughts for them, everything is going very well with you. Nothing can go wrong at all. Success is definite for you; there cannot be anything less than perfect. Don't talk anything lower than the highest vibration. Use the highest energy thoughts and words.

Our thoughts do not depend on how the situation is. Everything depends on how our thoughts are. So we should not make our thoughts dependent on the situation. We need to change the situation using our thoughts, because our thoughts create our world. Our thoughts create our feelings. Our thoughts affect our body. Our thoughts create our relationships. Our thoughts reach other people and create relationships. Our thoughts radiate into the environment and they create the world.

"There is nothing in this world that can trouble you more than your own thoughts."

---- Mahatma Buddha

Effective Communication

SMILE and RELAX

It kills Negativity =>develops=> HEALTHY RELASTIONSHIP

"Every Smile can touch somebody's Heart."

Alone I can say but together we can talk

Alone I can enjoy but together we can celebrate

Alone I can Smile but together we can laugh

That is the Beauty of Human Relationship

Without them we are nothing.

Communication is very vital for every relationship, whether it is with your wife, with your family, with your friends, or even in your surroundings where you reside. When your relations are healthy, Happiness will automatically come to you. In our daily hectic life, we are bond to time limit; we get very limited time to talk with our friends. For this our communication should be effective and polite.

Don't get so much reward by donating, as much as you get from your words. If your voice has sweetness, then the people who listen will give you blessings. Blessings are one of the best ways to get virtue.

For this and healthy relationship, three factors are very important:-

Forgiveness, Acceptance, Unconditional love

Forgiveness:

As you keep tolerating the hurts, your heart will be cleansed. You have to learn to keep forgiving.

We should learn the lesson, and keep them in mind so that people don't cheat you. At the same time you have to release the hurts that are present in your mind; in this way you are growing up spiritually. This is the most powerful way to grow up spiritually.

There are many people who have faith in God. But they don't forgive even God. They said, "Why did God do this to me?" They start wrong words even hatred towards God. At this stage God is kind to them in purifying their hearts. He will arrange for hurts. He will deliberately do something wrong with them in the path of love. You are continuing love Him and He is hurting you. A question will come in your mind, why? God is not in my favour, what is wrong with me? He is behaving adversely with me.

Answer is very simple, it is your test. God is taking the test of your true love. Now what is our role or duty at this point?

We must continue to love, that is true love. To reach the highest point of higher frequency, love means forgiveness ignoring all things which you had hurts by someone. Forgiveness means you don't harbor hurts within. Let's keep working on our spirituality. Let's move on until we can reach that platform where forgiveness becomes our nature. Because it is unproductive to keep resentments, no use to keep this thought in our mind which is going to hurt us. We should come to the point where forgiveness becomes a natural process and then we will be free from all tensions.

I am bending, because I want to be flexible. I want to be happy, I want to be healthy. I want to vibrate at high frequency. I have nothing to do with anyone.

Forgiveness is the foundation of meaningful, deep and true relationship. When you say sorry, it doesn't mean that you are wrong. It means that you value the person and the relationship more than being right. You have to choose what you do you want; being right or love? If you want love, sometimes you have say sorry, even you are right.

Because lack of forgiveness we will have to pay a tremendous price, how?

If you harbor resentment, it will create emotional conflicts; it will create inner imbalance. You have to face health issues and many other problems. Forgiveness is a gift that we bestow upon ourselves.

Acceptance:

Most of the people in the world don't accept the reality. They are in dark, they think that they are right and others are wrong. They consider themselves more superior. It is nothing; it is because of their **Ego.** Their expectations are so high. It should keep in mind that expectations create pressure. They always complaint that it is not right, it is wrong. It should be like this. They starts comparison; comparison with others which is the root cause of stress in mind. Mind is not free from negative emotions.

Acceptance means willingness to tolerate a difficult situation. Acceptance in human psychology is a person's assent to the reality of a situation, recognizing a process or condition without attempting to change it or protest it.

Simple solution: - Accept the things as they are. Accept another for who they are their faults and weaknesses. Let them do what they want. Don't try to mend the things. Do not advice. Advice may be given to those who really want to take your advice. It is a perfect world; we cannot change it. If you want any change, mend yourself. Transform your habit of criticism. Criticizing to anyone leads to conflicts.

When something unpredictable happens, we start complaining and over thinking it. At this difficult moment of your life, you need to live with it. It is hard to practice acceptance when you deeply wish things different. But truth is, sometimes we cannot change the reality, even if we try. Let's turn around and see how many other doors we have open.

Accept the world as it is. This world is as it is for all of us. It is up to you how you wish to see it will determine your level of happiness.

We need to cultivate the ability to truly accept whatever comes and embrace it. In this universe, nothing is permanent, everything changes, and of course, a lot of things can happen that that transfers your life and leaves an impact your life.

You know, life never moves on a single track, it brings many challenges and these challenges are not easy to accept and embrace them. But we start cultivating acceptance in our mind right now, we'll likely cope with future crises in a different way and view them from a different perspective. If we resist and fight, we'll generate a lot of turbulence in our mind. We need to accept things as they are. This is the way you can make your life flow smoothly.

I'll not hesitate to mention an example of my close relative regarding to acceptance. I have already mentioned that life brings many challenges. My wife's sister had only son and he was lost in an accident. The death of dear one they loved was a great challenge for them, and it was not easy to embrace when they were suffering and wishing those things would have never happened. But if they started cultivating acceptance in their lives right then, they coped with future crises in a different way and viewed them from a different perspective. They accepted instead or resisting, but in the present moment it was very difficult to accept and they accepted things as they are. That's the way you can make your life flow smoothly instead of roughly.

From this incident of my life I have learned the true power of acceptance.

Try to learn true power of acceptance. Reject the option of judge what happens to you. Instead, believe that everything happens for a reason and better things will always follow. That is the beginning of true acceptance. When you have learnt this, you definitely will agree with Buddha's Advice:

Don't feel alone there is always someone who silently cares for you.

There are **two ways** out of **a problem**:

1. **Accept what's happening.**
2. **Fight against it.**

Your option is to choose the **first way**. See positive and choose a peaceful state of mind, which is a helpful tool in all aspects of life.

The second option is miserable, and struggle against the universe. Reject this option. Practicing acceptance prepares you to live in this changing world, where you never know what's going to happen next. Acceptance is the right path to move on our life.

This is beautiful line given by a great man:-

"God grant me the serenity to accept the things I cannot change."

Unconditional Love:

Unconditional Love is affection without any limitations or love without any condition. If you commit to loving God unconditionally, then you can rest assured that God is actively causing everything around you to work together for your good.

It is caring about another person's happiness without demanding for any benefits for themselves.

Love means your feelings and emotions. As you observe that emotions and feelings are changed with the course of time, but unconditional love is true and everlasting. It is love without strings attached. You don't base it on what someone does for you in return. You simply love them and want nothing in return more than their happiness. Prime example of Unconditional Love is your family and your children.

There are some ways you can how to love; practice them and change your life for the achievement of happiness.

1. Give importance to yourselves and unconditionally to yourselves:

Sometimes is come to notice that you are constantly pleasing others and you are lacking self-love. In this point change you, give yourself Unconditionally Love first and the rest will come.

2. With small and simple act everyday:

There are many ways in your daily life; you can act in such a way which will promote you for Unconditional Love. If you across a sick person and he is in need of your help. This is the best opportunity in the field of unconditional love. One day I left my home for my office, an aged man came to me and asked me to drop me sick mother in nearby hospital. This man was unknown to me and only few minutes were left to report my duty hours. Without wasting a single minute I took them to hospital in my own vehicle and I informed my office for coming late.

Do something every day and I promise – even though you don't want anything in return. In this way you'll get a huge amount of pleasure and happiness just doing a simple act and giving Unconditional Love.

3. **Show love to all even to those who show negative towards you:**

In your surroundings, there are some people of negative nature. Why is it so? It is because of lack of knowledge and these people lack something in their own life that prevents them from truly loving themselves. If you see this before you react, put yourself in unconditional love before them. It is here where you decide to give Unconditional Love and give it more frequently. Being this way will provide a good pay off for these people around you, but most importantly for you too.

4. **Be Cool and Relax:**

Everyone knows that pain and relief are the part of life; they are two sides of a coin. After every pain, there is a light in the life and that is the opportunity to grow. Pain and growth goes side by side and shielding them from this is not love, if you only set out to make them feel satisfied and happy all the time you will do more than good. Let them experience pain so that they will find this own way and grow them at their own pace. In every time and every situation, it is my humble opinion, be cool and relax.

5. **Adapt to new situation:**

Take a smartly decision in every new situation that comes along. There is no fixed rule for unconditional love; you can apply it as per the situation and person by person.

6. Unconditional Love doesn't depend upon your feeling:

Love is not how you feel, it depends how you act. How you feel it is more than how you act in response of a situation. Your action will determine your happiness and bring pleasure in your life.

7. Learn forgiveness and practically apply:

Keep silence and forgive others is a beautiful gift. I have already discussed in detail in the topic of forgiveness.

8. Detach from the Outcome

Relinquish your rigid attachment to a specific result and live in the wisdom of uncertainty. Attachment is based on fear and insecurity, while detachment is based on the unquestioning belief in the power of your true Self. Intend for everything to work out as it should, then let go and allow opportunities and openings to come your way.

There are **many ways for promoting unconditional love**. I have mentioned only few of them.

By promoting these three factors **(Forgiveness, Acceptance and Unconditional Love),** we can reach to World Peace.

First you have to work hard to build your inspiration in the field of these three factors, thus your behavior will become a part a part of you by repeated practice. You have the choice and willpower to reject the other options. Then it becomes a way natural way of your life.

Love, your relationship and your communication is more important than money. You work day and night to provide for yourself and your family. Without love there is little to inspire you to work harder or to have nicer things. There is also no one to whom you can leave the things you have worked hard for in life, and you can't take them with you when you pass away. Your relationship and your behaviour will be remembered.

We need to encourage others how to recognize the opportunities for unconditional love that leads to a happy and peaceful life. The choice to lead peaceful life definitely promotes interpersonal skills for dealing with conflict and friction that will arise with family and friends.

Education and Compassion

There is No Class to teach how we should speak but the way we speak definitely decides Our Class

Modern India's education is the objective thinking of western education that is why modern existing education is very much oriented to material education. Every education system is creating materialistic culture; the people pay more attention material values.

In the modern age our life is very easy; because modernization and economic competition in the world market and a high degree of scientific and technological knowledge have provided comforts and fulfilled our daily needs. The emphasis today is on material development, production of a large variety of consumer goods and on raising economic standards. This has led to greater attention on education in technical subjects that provide immediate access to the job market. Scientific and technical study may increase a students' knowledge of formulae and sharpen his memory in the field new researches.

However, without learning to apply the powers of reasoning and analysis to subjects like language, literature, social science, philosophy, history and political science, students are inadequately prepared for the breadth and depth of human life. There is a real danger of preoccupation with consumerism, and of finer feelings being overtaken by greed.

Today education in human and moral values has been ignored, disregarded and largely considered irrelevant as a preparation for life. Countries may produce well-trained scientist, engineers, doctors, lawyers, administrators, business executives, artists etc., however, society shows increasing signs of suffering from the consequent loss of human touch which have been displaced by materialism. As a result of this students are not aware of moral values.

Generations coming from this education eventually create materialistic culture. So people pay attention towards materialistic values. No doubt, we should pay attention to material value; because the whole world is after the materialistic culture. Every nation is putting its best efforts in the field of advancement; new researches are being done for making life easy in the matter of physical comforts. So everyone is chasing the wrong one and ignoring the right one.

It is a matter of great concern that corruption, bribery and nepotism at various levels, even in every sphere of our daily routine, in the world are prevalent despite laws against them. Corruption means to use or be willing to use political or social power to perform dishonest or illegal actions in return for money or some advantage. The root of this attitude is greed and this practice is continuously going on.

Today's reality--- Inner values are being ignored. Happiness is a part of our inner experience which must develop within our mind. If we are having too many facilities, in return too much anger and anxiety is inside. Then such people come across some mental level problem. Then they start reading books and try to find out the way of happiness. Now time has come we should pay equal attention for our inner values and material values; keeping the balance. Education is the key factor to inculcate the inner values. The basic question is that what to do in our education system. How to develop inner values?

Answer is simple, special attention must be paid in our education system; hygiene of emotions, then we can tackle with emotions. Most of things come through actions. Take the example of Compassion, which comes through action. In one session, **H.H. Dalai Lama described the example of his mother**.

In real sense, mother is the first teacher of a child. Very early in the childhood I (H.H. Dalai Lama) could learn and adopted Compassion through action of my mother. He told that there was a famine, people started to move in the search of food. A group of people came to our village and my mother immediately came out of the house to welcome them. Without wasting a single moment, she started bringing everything which she had in our house. We all brothers and sisters helped her in this noble cause. Compassion comes through actions.

H.H.Dalai Lama stressed on compassion and in every talk his main objective was how to build compassion. For inner peace, more compassion able attitude, regardless attitude from others which reduces enemies. He said, "Real seed of compassion came to me from my mother. I can't describe her kindness attitude. Her kindness was greater than my teachers."

Every woman has potential of this seed of compassion and by utilizing this potential for their children, and then the way of life will change. Consider all brothers and sisters, develop this attitude. They also deserve happy life. Develop the sense of concern to everybody, ------this result no enemy. If there is no enemy results no fear. Our extreme self-centered attitude leads to lack of affection, lack of brotherhood ship and lack of compassion. Think of one, don't care others. This kind of motivation is unrealistic and wrong action; as a result there are unwanted problems, eventually created by us. And there is mental projected fear that transfers unhappiness in Mind. Sometimes it grows Anger and anger brings suspicious. Suspicious destroys trust--------that results you feel distance from others. 90% of negativity comes from suspicious which is mental projected. As a result of this violence is sure.

So, we really need of healthy proper mental attitude. It is very important to more attention on inner values.

On the other hand compassion brings inner strength, compassion brings trust, and compassion brings openness; that brings more friends and more affection from others. Compassionate mind really gets feeling you are surrounding by friends, full affection that brings inner calmness of peace and more happiness. Compassion brings calmness and calmness provides good brain which can judge good and bad. When there is anger in the mind/brain; your subconscious mind is in emotional pain, anxiety, depression or stress. It will not function normally. You cannot take the right decision in any area of life and a result of this wrong decision. Wrong decision is definitely harmful to all, all mean yourself as well as society. Neutral mind opens potential of judgments. Our physical health is also depending on inner peace.

Scientists are also in the opion of basic nature of the human being is more compassionate, because we are social animals. So compassionate for peace of mind, you can be happy person. Money, power and fan will not help you to bring peace. So pay more attention to compassion, and then it is possible to bring peace. Promote humanity; humanity comes from inner peace. Take a beautiful example of little children. You see children play together, doesn't care about different faith, different religion, and keeping smile on their face. We need that spirit; this type of spirit must remain our hearts.

I am proud of my country. In my country, India over 3000 years, we are committed to **Ahinsha**. This is the right way to reach compassionate. As per statement of H.H. Dalai Lama, 'I feel sense of oneness in seven billion people. When I go any part of the world I feel same as in my home Dhramshala, I am not something special. I always keep smiling, I don't need formalities. I always create friendly atmosphere. I never think that I am Dalai Lama.'

By practicing this we can reduce self-centered attitude.

One formula of Inner Values should be taught in all schools and colleges and expressed the opinion that if it were properly taught it would so revolutionize the entire educational system that a change could be brought in the coming years.

According to H.H. Dalai Lama,

If you want others to be happy, built compassion: if you want to be happy; practice compassion.

The Dalai Lama's words are instructive because they refer to the emotional benefits of compassion to both the giver and recipient. In other words, the rewards of practicing compassion work both ways.

First we understand the meaning of 'compassion', various definitions of compassion have been proposed by researchers and philosophers. But I consider this view of **Cassell (2009)** very important for compassion; he has reported the following three requirements for compassion:

1) "That the troubles that evoke our feelings are serious;"

2) "That the sufferers' troubles not be self-inflicted— that they be the result of an unjust fate;" and

3) "We must be able to picture ourselves in the same predicament".

As such, compassion is not an automatic response to another's plight; it is a response that occurs only when the situation is perceived as serious, unjust and relatable. It requires a certain level of awareness, concern and empathy.

Consistent with the above definition, seeing a homeless man on the sidewalk will register differently depending upon how this situation is uniquely perceived by passersby. The amount of compassion elicited by others will be dependent upon how serious his situation is deemed, as well as the perceived degree of fault attributed to him for his predicament.

Psychologists are also interested in the role of compassion towards oneself. When individuals view their own behaviors and shortcomings without compassion, they may ruminate about their faults and inadequacies in such a way that erodes self-esteem and happiness.

Because of the importance of self-kindness and -forgiveness to mental health, the concept of 'self-compassion' is occurring more often in the psychological literature.

According to the Dalai Lama:

Each of us in our own way can try to spread compassion into people's hearts. Western civilizations these days place great importance on filling the human 'brain' with knowledge, but no one seems to care about filling the human 'heart' with compassion. This is what the real role of religion is.

A strong emphasis on the attainment of knowledge in materialist field except one field (compassion)— with minimal attention given to the teaching of compassion.

According to the H.H. Dalai Lama:

We are preventing the youth from becoming sensitive to the vital domains of life --------empathy, reflexivity and communion.

Communion means sharing of intimate thoughts on a mental and spiritual level.

Schooling is the important stage of life. Schooling education can make a difference. Our focus is drawing upon ancient Indian traditions to provide direction for the future.

Objective of Education to educate teachers as to how they can formally inculcate Human Values such as:

1. **Respect**
2. **Honesty**
3. **Compassion**
4. **Patience**
5. **Humility**
6. **A sense of responsibility**

These values would help students become educated in true sense for a better society. These are basic needs in the welfare of the society as well as world's happiness.

Teachers have a significant role in shaping the future generations.

There should be coordination between the ancient Indian education and the modern one. True education comes when it is accompanied by spiritual knowledge

Change your vision and your vision will change you.

Education is basically a process of nurturing, developing and shaping the thought process of children.

Entire universe is suffering from an acute crisis of diminishing moral values. This is a very dangerous situation in the present scenario. In the world there is one thing is common that there is increase in physically, emotionally and mentally problems among our youths. It is because of our education. True education consists of spiritual education.

If we go back to our history, our country was rich in teaching of spiritual values. In ancient India there were Gurukuls, the pupil had to spend twelve or more years to learn ethics; moral values and spiritual values along with physical task. Now we are in such environment where these values are being ignored. There are many problems (anxiety, stress, fear etc.) being faced by our young generation. Studies have shown that serious mental, emotional and physical consequences such as depression, anxiety and the feeling that your life lacks meaning and purpose, as well as the loss of valuable connectedness with family and friends become high prices to pay in future.

Everyone is in search of peace, a place where there is no stress, a place of relax. I have above mentioned six elements of human values and our passing out students are lacking behind of these elements. A lack of these values force them to do something wrong in their life. It is the main reason they show a lackadaisical attitude towards their place of work. After sometimes they feel there is something lacking in their life.

To overcome this ethical crisis, it is necessary to educate the present generation in spiritual values. Spiritual values means moral values and this will be a correct approach to globalization. It will automatically enrich the person's personality.

The very purpose of Education is to improve the Quality of Life, not based on knowledge alone but value-based education and knowledge. Not merely believing in skills for earning a living, Education also is for life.

We must be committed to meet the challenge by promoting Values and Spirituality through education and research work, so as to arouse the divine consciousness of the teacher and student.

Education in values can make a significant impact on many of social ills that exist due to lack of values. At present, most people assume that corruption, bribery and nepotism are part of life. Education in values, through many channels of communication, will increase awareness and provide people of all ages as well as social groups with the necessary tools and skills to resist pressure to conform to such practices.

When education in values and spirituality is integrated into technical education programs and provided to both genders equally, it results in more balanced individuals who are properly equipped for civil life.

Education in human values and spirituality contributes to shifting deeply entrenched social attitudes, which are antagonistic to women and people of lower caste who legally have the same rights as everyone else. Education in values also boosts the confidence of socially disadvantaged individuals and inspires them to claim their rights.

A teacher has to understand this condition and along-with his regular task of imparting knowledge and skills, correct the mind set and view point of the society. **The day is not far when the question "where have the values gone?" will not remain in books.**

As teachers, we are supposed the act of gaining knowledge from all possible corners and sources and keep the students concerned and concentrated to their prime concern of gaining knowledge for positive self-development.

Suggestion:

I believe that we should pay more attention towards educating hearts, that is, students should be taught love, kindness, peace, compassion, self-control, simplicity and tolerance. I am a fan of social sensibility and moral education. I believe that in this era, we should take the initiative to educate the heart and brain. This effort is necessary in the field of education, which emphasizes on mental and emotional cleanliness and through which the students develop healthy mind. This education be made compulsory from Kindergarten to Senior Secondary schools, even be continue to college level and university level. I believe that India is the only country which has the ability to connect its ancient tradition with modern education. Therefore it should work to bring harmony between ancient and modern education. We can take such an example from Tibetan's culture. The knowledge and cultural tradition that they got from India during thousands of years, they have accumulated.

The best way to impart this education, there should be a period of thirty minutes of every class up to the standard of High School once a week. It is my personal suggestion. All teachers are supposed to gain knowledge of moral and spiritual values from all possible sources, either spending time in library or availing online/internet facilities. In this way we will achieve our goal of inculcating the values of peace, love, compassion, kindness, simple living and high thinking among the coming generation.

Moksha (Salvation)

Now I come to the main question; this question is very important and related to everyone, related to seven billion people. These people belong to any of religion, no question of religion. What is the ultimate aim of our birth on this earth?

The mother gives birth to a child and child comes to this earth. He is ignorant of real aim of this birth on the earth. He starts to learn whatever he observes surrounding him. He observes the material world.

The ultimate goal of our birth on this earth is to get Moksha (not repeated circle of birth---again and again).

Moksha, also called vimoksha, vimukti and mukti, is a term in Hinduism, Buddhism, Jainism and Sikhism for various forms of emancipation, enlightenment, liberation, and release. In its soteriological and eschatological senses, it refers to freedom from saṃsāra, the cycle of death and rebirth.

Moksha is a concept associated with saṃsāra (birth-rebirth cycle). This release was called moksha, nirvana, kaivalya, mukti and other terms in various Indian religious traditions. Eschatological ideas evolved in Hinduism.

Most Hindu traditions consider moksha the ultimate goal of life. The other three goals are considered temporary but necessary stepping-stones towards eternal liberation.

The main differences of opinion Centre on the precise nature of moksha. Although practically all schools consider it a state of unity with God, the nature of such unity is contested. The advaita traditions say that moksha entails annihilation of the soul's false sense of individuality and realization of its complete non-difference from God. The dualistic traditions claim that God remains ever distinct from the individual soul. Union in this case refers to a commonality of purpose and realization of one's spiritual nature (brahmand) through surrender and service to the Supreme Brahman (God).

1. **For most Hindus, moksha is the highest goal.**
2. **Moksha means release from samsara.**
3. **Moksha is achieved through union with God.**

In the previous chapters I have discussed and tried to clarify many points. For our survival worldly things are also very important, success in every sphere is also important. In the chapter of Thought, it has been clarified how to reach your goal which you have set. In this chapter I'll touch some important points which may help to reach our goal to Moksha.

It is very important give more stress on this line. Mold your Body and your Mind in such a way that they must be in your control, don't allow them freedom otherwise they will become the masters of your of your Soul. Because those who committed to excellence in every little act of theirs, they control their body and mind as per the direction of Soul.

For achieving any success there is one more major hindrance that is Laziness. You have the choice and willpower to reject the lazy option; and be energetic. If you control both mind and body it conquers the factor of laziness.

The mind is made of the material energy and it has three characteristics--------**GOODNESS, PASSION and IGNORANCE.**

When the mind is in Goodness, you think the human form is so precious. I have golden chance, I must reach the goal. Hence you are inspired.

When the mind is in the mode of Passion, you think both materialistic world and something to worship God. It is in your mind that the worldly things are also important and must be achieved before God.

When your mind in third mode, mode of Ignorance, you start thinking nobody has ever seen God. Many people don't believe in God. Why is it that I have to believe in Him? Your enthusasm gets shattered. As long as you are under the influence of materialistic things, it will happen. But you don't need to let it be like this.

Sadhana means to fight it and to go beyond this. So how do you build up your enthusiasm? Bring the right knowledge to your intellect. Daily Sadhana is important. It is food for soul. You cannot neglect food for the body. Similar something is required for Soul. Sadhana is more important than eating. Bring this knowledge to your intellect and then force the mind up to the level of inspiration. You have to work on correcting the intellect and aligning the mind. When you again and again, it will become natural to them. First, you have to work hard to build your inspiration, and then it becomes naturally. After sometime it becomes so natural you cannot act any other way.

Now, how do this?

Our goal is to purify the mind. You, purify the mind by attaching it to the all pure God. Purify your mind and the subconscious mind. You, make them Divine. It is question how to make them divine?

For one week, you must be very conscious to watch, read and listen what you want to become. Cleanse your mind and soul, and thereafter only consume pure information. In this way we don't have to worry about positive thinking. Positive thinking will become the natural way of living.

You can visualize the image of your God (it may be of your Lord or your Ishta Dev). The power of visualization can help you accomplish our ultimate goal in life which purifies the mind. To do that, you should meditate on the image of God, which is pure and divine.

First thing in the morning should be pure powerful information. It includes spiritual knowledge, messages of God, wisdom----------mind with the right emotional diet. Thinking will automatically change and right thoughts will automatically get created. This is the method by which we can switch to a pure **EMOTIONAL DIET**.

The power visualization can help us accomplish our ultimate goal which is to purify the mind. To do that, you should meditate on the image of God, who is pure and divine. Think about the goal you want to achieve in your life. Make it a habit to visualize yourself in the state where you accomplished your goal. Do this, first in the morning after you wake up and every night before you go to sleep. You will find yourself much inspired to work on your goal and it will result in the faster achievement of the goal.

Make yourself **emotionally** strong. So for this one hour in the morning let us stay away from such information's----------information of criticism, information of discontentment and humiliation, information of other relating to negative approach. Choose the information of higher energy, pure powerful information-----wisdom, spiritual knowledge, message of God which will make you emotionally strong.

I'll also touch the point of Meditation. Meditation has a vital role to purify the mind. In every day especially morning time, all information we listen, we read and we watch should be of spiritual wisdom (higher energy). This is the right way of shifting to positive thinking. As the soul keeps getting filled with spiritual wisdom, with experience a beautiful relationship with God. This is Meditation, means connecting with Supreme Power, connecting with God; and experience a very beautiful personal relationship with God. We share everything with God; we take God's advice in every step of your working. In this way we can develop a personal relationship with God through which we communicate all our feelings to God. We will listen to whatever God wants to guide us. Our life will become easy if we take advice from God.

In this way of daily routine, there is a transformation in our self with the changes in our routine work. Our desires start reducing and our expectations come down. We will remain stable and peaceful. We will calm internally, crisis is outside; it will continue to remain outside. Care and Compassion will become a part of our daily routine.

There is a significant change in our world; state of mind will be better; physical health will be better; relationship with all will be beautiful; we will start experiencing all this.

Here I'll touch one more important point which also helps in achieving the goal, which is **'Law of Attraction'**.

This 'law of attraction' has been explained long ago by the spiritual guru. Today's Scientist also defines this law. If we understand this then we can achieve the goal in life.

It is important to understand how to apply this rule in life.

Everything we want is attracted towards us. We must act after what we think. 'So people act as per they want, they get that'.

But it does not happen many times. We don't always get what we want, why is this so?

1. If our thinking is not pure.

2. If our thoughts are not good

This happens because of our dedication towards our thinking. Two important things are must for this.

So even by doing karma we can't get it.

That's why two things need to happen.

1. **Intelligent thinking**
2. **Good deeds**

Nothing happens just by thinking:

Thinking should be pure; resolution should be firm and deep,

Karma must be right.

One should have courage to go till the last path.

Our thinking is our beginning. Our thinking should not be mixed. For us to do anything, we should know from within ourselves that what we are thinking, whether it is not for a moment, whether we are meant for that, it is important to know. Mere thinking does nothing; a thought paves the way for you. That's why it is very important to have calmness and stability in our mind. Your thinking can attract things towards you and action can make it easier to achieve. Your determination and action keep you under control in achieving your goal.

There are **three unsolved questions**; nobody abled to answer these questions, no research work has done in this field. These are:-

1. Where does the Soul go after the death?

2. How many days/months/years to take rebirth on the earth?

3. Is it possible to become the permanent part of Divine Soul? It is the stage of Moksha.

I discussed these questions with many people, but I could not have a satisfactory answer. Some has suggested me that when your desires are zero and you are detached from this materialistic world, then we are near to Moksha. This is not my opinion; it is all which I had discussion with learned personalities.

Ultimate way to reach

First step is self-analysis. It is very important to witness everything minutely. There are important questions:-

What am I doing?

Which direction my life is going?

What am I thinking? --------Positive or Negative

What type of faith I am creating?

And which way my present life is running?

This is your self-analysis. Try to come out of this. If you are able to evaluate these questions, then you are on the right path. Your vision should be holistic; a holistic approach to living.

A holistic approach means to provide support that looks at the whole person, not just their mental health needs. The support should also consider their physical, emotional, social and spiritual wellbeing.

As the evaluation is over; now come to real approach in the following way:-

1. Create a thought what I want my life to be.
2. I don't create the thought what my life is.
3. I create the thought what my life should be.

In other way a simple way to understand:-

Never wait for a Perfect Moment; just take a Moment, and Make it Perfect.

I know the equation my life does not create thought; my thought creates my life.

Thought becomes reality.

Faith is the main chief in the mind. When faith is blended with the vibration of thought, the subconscious mind instantly picks up the vibration, translates into spiritual reality.

Faith is nothing; it is the state of mind which may be created, by repeated of orders given to subconscious mind.

When a man first comes into contact with some new thing, he abhors it. If he remains in contact with the same for a time, he becomes accustomed to it, and endures it. If he remains in contact with it for long, he finally embraces it, and becomes induced by it. This is true that any impulse of thought which is repeatedly passed on to the subconscious mind is finally accepted. In this way faith is developed, where it does not already exist. It may be understood by a beautiful example, take a case of a new born child, when he is two or three years old. He tries to notice all the activities as well as other things which are happening around him. In almost all families there are religious rituals daily. This child observes their elders and tries to fellow them, in this way his faith is developed for religion.

Faith is a force which gives life, power and action to the impulse of thought. Let's consider the power of faith. Take the well-known example of the person in the world, Mahatma Gandhi. His desires were very few and he had very things; he had two or three dhoties, he ate in a wooden bowl with wooden spoon. He had no money, he had no home, and he lived in a kutia. But he did have the power of faith. In this man the world had one of the most astounding examples known to civilization, of the possibilities of faith.

How did he come by that power?

He created it out of his understanding of the principle of Faith, and through his ability to transplant that faith into minds of two hundred million people and these two hundred million minds to coalesce and move in unison, as a single mind.

Someone has truly said, "Faith in God and do the right." Faith in God is the first step in the right way of our journey. Many people do not have patience; they cannot wait for a specific period.

Having faith in God, we prayer. Prayers are the strongest medium of connecting with Supreme Power (with Godly Power). Human hearts can connect with God by prayer. We can share our feelings by connecting to purest heart. By devotion a source of energy we believe is gained from God as a blessing in various forms. Always use God beliefs and devotion to reach our goal.

For spiritual growth is to know truly what you REALLY and Truly want in life. It may seem to you that you want something, but your Sub-Conscious mind may be communicating something else. Your actual seeking is held in the Sub-Conscious mind and not the Conscious mind. With meditation you have to first find out what you truly desire and then work on materializing it.

I have learned three important things from spiritual persons; these are

1. **Shravan (Listen)**: - means to listen. Try to listen only positive talks open your ears to listen relevant material which is your business and positive. Avoid irrelevant.

2. **Sankirtan (Talk)**: - means you speak be positive. Your reply will not hurt anybody. When you talk

in a way no one will criticize you. In your every talk there must be a message of God.

3. **Manan (Thinking in Mind)**: - means positive thoughts in your mind. In every thought there must be positive thinking; no room for negative thinking. Cement your thoughts of thinking in the positive direction.

As I have already mentioned in pervious chapter that most of the people are not happy, even not healthy because of our own thinking. Eighty percent of the sick people are of their thinking. One thing keep in mind that overthinking is the biggest root cause of your unhappiness. Whatever they think starts materialize. Many people are in the grip of psychosomatic disorder. Psychosomatic illness originates from emotional stress and manifests in the body which may be in form of physical pain and some other symptoms. By the result of this psychosomatic factor, immune system of the body becomes weakened. It may be cured. People experience different types of illnesses due to psychic stress. Medication is the best way to release stress. You, yourself as much as anybody in the entire universe, deserve your love and affection. Give love and receive love is the key factor of stress free life.

According to Swami Vivekananda,

"You have to grow from inside out. None can teach you, none can make you spiritual. There is no other teacher but your own Soul."

Life is a circle happiness; hard times and good times. If you are going through hard times, have faith that good times are on the way. It will come definitely; on one can stop it. Believe in yourself. Success is not the key to happiness, but happiness is the key to success. If you love what you are doing, you will success.

There are different paths; ways and activities that bring you close to supreme power (God). In Hinduism religion, it is a very important word 'PUNYA'.

Punya Karma means the activities of pious; activities of 'saintly', virtue, 'holy', 'sacred', 'pure', 'good', 'meritorious', 'virtuous', 'righteous'.

Actions performed as per the authorization and under guidance of the vedic literatures is known as karma and the result of such action is piety. Piety means Punya. Punya offers a lot of happiness, peace, good parentage, heavenly life, good education, money, beauty etc. Work hard in the field of your interest in order of build up a better Karma. This way you will be close to God and you can achieve a favourable future rebirth.

There are some ways by which one can get Punya. It is not very difficult to move on these ways; but there is urgent need of your faith and your willpower to move on this road. Following are two very important requirements:

1. **Nirmal Man (Refined Heart ----Crystal Clear)**

Transparent Picture gives an idea of what I want to tell you

Nirmal Man means no negativity in your heart.

2. **Shuddh Bhavana (Pure Intention)**

When there is a positive thinking, above mentioned both things can only be satisfied. In this way you cannot think anything wrong; you will think good for others and will do the same. Many people are in the opinion of this thinking and they suggest the way of Punya by adopting the way of positive thinking. Efforts are made not hurt the emotions of human beings, even not religious emotions. When you remark to anyone and your remarks hurt their feelings. This way is not of pure intention. By practicing of Shuddh Bhavana (Pure Intention), you can increase your vibrational frequency.

In this universe many people complain of wish, they usually say every day I pray to God and bow before Him to fulfill my wish, even then I am not succeeded. What is wrong with me? They start saying no God is in the universe. But they forget above mentioned two things. They may be lack of these two things. Their vibrational frequency is of lower. It is my humble suggestion that increase your vibrational frequency to higher point. Without having them you cannot reach to your goal. I have already talked about (in the previous chapter) adopt three things (Forgiveness, Acceptance and Unconditional Love) in your life. By adopting these three important things, your heart will be transparent and crystalline. Your intention towards others will be pure. In this way you are at point of higher vibrational frequency. You are always positive and energetic. When you are positive, your thinking is of higher.

A very simple concept, yet so true: that which we manifest is before us; we are the creators of our own destiny. Be it through intention or ignorance, our successes and our failures have been brought on by none other than ourselves.

"Believing in negative thoughts is the single greatest obstruction to success."

Intention is one of the most powerful forces. What you mean when you do a thing will always determine the outcome. This creates the world.

"All great acts are ruled by intention. What you mean is what you get."

"Powerful words come with powerful intent. Where you have passion, strength, courage, and determination you can accomplish anything!"

"When your intentions are pure, so too will be your success."

Every journey begins with the first step of articulating the intention, and then becoming the intention.

"The sages of India observed thousands of years ago that our destiny is ultimately shaped by our deepest intentions and desires. The classic Vedic text known as the Upanishads declares, "You are what your deepest desire is. As your desire is, so is your intention. As your intention is, so is your will. As your will is, so is your deed. As your deed is, so is your destiny."

An intention is a directed impulse of consciousness that contains the seed form of that which you aim to create. Like real seeds, intentions can't grow if you hold on to them. Only when you release your intentions into the fertile depths of your consciousness can they grow and flourish.

Intention is much more powerful when it comes from a place of contentment than if it arises from a sense of lack or need. Stay centered and refuses to be influenced by other people's doubts or criticisms. Your higher self knows that everything is all right and will be all right, even without knowing the timing or the details of what will happen.

One of the most effective tools we have is meditation. Meditation takes you beyond the ego-mind into the silence and stillness of pure consciousness. This is the ideal state in which to plant your seeds of intention.

Once you're established in a state of restful awareness, release your intentions and desires. The best time to plant your intentions is during the period after meditation, while your awareness remains centered in the quiet field of all possibilities. After you set an intention, let it go—simply stop thinking about it. Continue this process for a few minutes after your meditation period each day.

Meditation is a powerful tool that it can make all your worries disappear. Silence is necessary to control the senses. Through the meditation process, you can observe your mind and focus your attention. This meditation does not belong to any religion, but is an ocean of knowledge of our ancestors, based on very scientific principles. This meditation and healing reaches deep down to the root cause of your unhappiness or suffering and heals (releases) it, and immediately there is a positive transformation in your life. Meditation not only relaxes you completely, and heals you, but also brings good changes in your personality; you need to experience it to believe in it.

I'll give an example of my own experience of my life; I have seen the person of malafied intention. But they always used to go religious places, continuously praying to God in the morning and evening. Even that they are not happy. In the last time of their life they had to suffer more. On this my observation I talked to many people so that I would get exact answer. Then I talked to an old man and he was well known the whole story of a woman. She used to go temple every morning and spent a lot of time in worship God. At last time of her life she had very much suffering due to health problem. Her family members were praying to God for her Mukti (praying for her last breath). But it took several months. The old man told me that he had seen her and observed her activities during her life period and it was noticed by me that her intention towards others (except her family members) was malafied (bad intention). In every time her intention was negative. She never had positive thinking. He also narrated the example of a man (who was the neighbour of that woman). That man very rarely went to temple in his life time and he did spend very less time to worship God. At last time of life he was physically well and he had left this world within seconds without any physically disease. Nobody believed that he was no more. He had no suffering during his life period relating to his health problem and societal adjustment issue. Why is it so? It is because of his pure intention. He had always positive thinking. He never had malafied intention.

These are examples of negative and positive thinking; malafied and pure intention. From these examples we can learn and modify our way of life.

Best way of getting **Punya (Virtue)**

Focus Your Attention in Positive Ways

There is another way. You can unite attention and intention to increase your well-being. There are some immediate and effective changes that you can incorporate immediately. At least once every day, try to do the following:

1. Be of service to another person. Give them your time, sympathy, and attention. Make them feel listened to and cared for.

2. Immerse yourself in nature and its healing influence, even if it means only a brief walk outside. As you walk, don't occupy yourself texting or talking. Let your attention be quietly captured by trees, grass, the sun, and the sky—whatever allows you to commune with nature.

3. Do something that comforts you. Do something that comforts someone else.

4. Find a source of inspiration. Whether it is art, music, or poetry, make it be something that touches you deeply. Encourage others also.

5. Do something that you enjoy and make you laugh; do something that makes others smile and cheerful.

6. Extend your appreciation to someone else.

Now you have a basis for using your attention in a positive way that enhances your well-being while avoiding the use of attention that increases stress. But there is one intention that goes even deeper, and if you adopt it, you will find that attention and intention have the power to transform of your life.

Be crystal clear in what you want. Cleanse your karmas and open the pathways to success, growth and spirituality. Be ascendant in spirituality. But after that, it is up to you to create and manifest. Learn to tap what you want and make your life beautiful. Believe that only good will happen to you.

Conclusion

In today's era man is surrounded by many problems, Even our youth have many problems like Stress, Anxiety and Depression. Today's youth is getting confused, why? Today's youth is not able to control the mind, but the path is being misguided. Most of your stress comes from the way you respond, not the way life is. Adjust your attitude, and all that extra stress is gone.

I tried to focus on moral values. I have also emphasized the importance of being silent. Silence is necessary to control the senses. Through the meditation process, you can observe your mind and focus your attention.

I have touched upon all these problems in this book and have tried to show some ways; and these ways are helpful to solve many problems. In this way you can get your goal. Emotions have a big role in our lives. Control your emotions and make your life easy. Theory of Let-Go is very helpful for attaining Happiness.

The goal of our birth is to attain salvation, for this there must be Happiness in our life. Without happiness, we cannot reach to our goal. By some simple steps in our life, by adopting simple way we can have a happy and peaceful life. A simple and disciplined life is the only way to attain our goal.

In this way you can get salvation

Based on what I have written in this book, I have come to the conclusion that there are three types of people in this world. I'm going to tell you about them.

First, those people who is limited only to earn and eat in life.

Earning and eating is the goal of their life. These people do not have any concern from the rest of the world; their life is like an animal. Why did they come to this earth? To earn and eat is the only their goal in life, nothing else more than that. They understand that life meant for this.

This life is useless; none can expect anything from them.

Second, those people who earn money only in life. These people firmly believe in money. They think that everything is money and happiness is in money.

Their entire energy, their entire efforts, even their entire life is spent in the pursuit of earning money. Money is everything for them. Consider it to be the success of life. These people have too much self-centered attitude and ignore the needs of others and only do what's best for them. They make money in life, consider it as life itself. More money is the success of their life. How to earn more money is the goal of their life. These people spend their earned money only for themselves or their family. They don't get out of this and don't want to help anyone. To raise maximum facilities for oneself and take advantage of pleasures for oneself is their motive. Their thinking is only about themselves, this is the ego. These people are full of ego.

Third are those people, whose life is absolutely different and beautiful life, meant for special purpose? They look at life for meaningful purpose. They spend their lives in the service of people. They want to lay down their lives in the service of the people. They consider it as their religion. They spend their lives serving the people. They never lag behind in spending their all whatever they have in the welfare of society, it is their prime duty. They understand that life doesn't come again and again. Such persons do not think for themselves, they think for others. They feel joy in helping the needed person. They get everything even after losing everything. They consider rest of the world as one community and share common values and beliefs. We can share one planet and one future; we have a responsibility to each other, no matter where we live or how different our cultures are. This is significant life. We all should try for this life. Try for a **significant** and **meaningful** life, it should our thinking, so that **we'll be remembered even we are no more.**

www.ingramcontent.com/pod-product-compliance
Lightning Source LLC
LaVergne TN
LVHW061618070526
838199LV00078B/7329